# Creative
# VEGETARIAN
# Cooking

## LYNN BEDFORD HALL

Photography by Malcolm Dare

NEW
HOLLAND

First published in the UK in 1992 by
New Holland (Publishers) Ltd
37 Connaught Street, London W2 2AZ

ISBN 1 85368 184 9 (Hbk)
ISBN 1 85368 207 1 (Pbk)

Editors: Alison Leach, Sandie Vahl
Designers: Janice Evans and Joan Sutton
Cover design: Paul Wood
Photographer: Malcolm Dare
Food stylist: Georgia Shubitz
Phototypeset by Ace Filmsetting Ltd., Frome, Somerset
Printed and bound in Hong Kong by Leefung-Asco Printers Ltd

# CONTENTS

## Publisher's note

When using any recipe in this book, please follow either all the metric measures given or all the Imperial measures. Do not attempt to combine these, as they are not interchangeable.

## Author's acknowledgements

A book of this kind involves creative input from several people. In particular, I wish to thank Sandie Vahl for her amazing dedication, meticulous editing, and the endless hours of overtime she cheerfully contributed in order to get the book published on schedule; Malcolm Dare, who is responsible for the superb photographs, both on the cover and inside; and his talented and hard-working team — especially cook Mampula Swanepoel, and stylist Georgia Shubitz whose bubbling energy and enthusiasm produced such eye-catching compositions; Janice Evans and Joan Sutton for the exceptionally hard work they put into designing a bulky manuscript; Abdul Amien for the striking cover design; Linda de Villiers and George Vine for their encouragement and support in helping this book see the light of day.

Last, but definitely not least, thank you to my family who patiently have to help me test my efforts and have never once, when eating dishes created for this vegetarian book, put in a plea for meatballs.

## Photography acknowledgements

The publishers and photographer would like to thank the following for their contribution to the wonderful photographs in this book:
- [ ] Georgia Shubitz for styling the photographs
- [ ] Mampula Swanepoel for preparing and cooking the food
- [ ] Lucienne Vermeuelen for finding props
- [ ] Lee-Ann Edwards for her assistance in the studio
- [ ] Block & Chisel Interiors, Bric-A-Brac-Lane, Collectors Corner Antiques, Garlicks and Stuttafords for the loan of crockery
- [ ] Trend Textiles for the loan of fabric

**TERMINOLOGY**

The following list may help regarding minor variations in terminology and availability of some ingredients.

| | |
|---|---|
| Aubergines | Egg plants/Brinjals |
| Baby marrows | Zucchini |
| Cheese: | |
| low-fat soft | smooth cottage |
| Cream: | |
| single/double | standard |
| soured | sour |
| Cucumber | English cucumber |
| Marmite | Vegemite |
| Oregano | Origanum |
| Tomato passata | Tomato purée |
| Tomato purée | Tomato paste |

# PREFACE

*I* have written this book for a number of reasons, but mainly out of desperation. I am not a vegetarian, but I love vegetarian meals, I have a keen interest in wholefoods because their merits make such good sense, and I really enjoy dishes featuring grains and pulses in particular. But so many books on the subject — despite the excellence of their content — give a lot of space to simple things like wholewheat breads and fresh-fruit puddings. I wanted recipes with substance; meatless dishes which would fill people up and not leave hungry diners longing for chops or chicken. A tossed green salad served with bread is not a meal, and besides, people don't need a cookbook to tell them how to prepare a green salad. And so I have written this book, packed with hearty dishes, as a reference book for myself, and, I hope, for lots of others who are interested in cutting down on their intake of animal protein and stepping up on other, natural products.

My aim has been to create satisfying meals without meat or fish, with the emphasis on unprocessed foods, to serve on a couple of nights each week. This will involve you, not only in checking the label on everything you buy, but also in a lot of washing, chopping and cooking of vegetables; soaking of beans; straining, steaming and simmering. You could end up wishing you were simply frying a steak and had never bought this book. Your family might even leave home. So why persevere? For two reasons: firstly, for most people it is becoming an economic impossibility to eat red meat, chicken or fish every day; and secondly, there's the healthy spin-off that comes with eating less fat and sugar, while stepping up on fibre, and using carbohydrates for fuel. This is not a crankish approach. Obesity, high cholesterol levels, diabetes, and all sorts of other ailments are often caused by eating too much of the wrong foods, too often. Changing one's eating habits can change one's whole life.

But fanaticism is a mistake. Becoming a committed vegetarian means knowing your oats; it's an involved and scientific way of eating which has many pitfalls for the uninitiated, such as a possible lack of protein. One has to be on the ball when it comes to combining foods to achieve a nutritional balance — like always serving pulses with whole grains, for example — and I don't claim to be an expert in this sphere. With pasta dishes, particularly, a proper balance can be a problem. But it cannot be denied that more and more people are looking to a style of wholesome eating in which processed foods, with all their colorants, flavourings and other additives, play no part.

There is no need to go overboard; food is interesting and exciting, and eating should be a pleasure. To deny yourself the enjoyment of sampling all kinds of foods can simply stamp you as an eccentric and leave you undernourished. Be sensible, and be moderate. If you suddenly have the urge to eat chicken in cream, or herby, garlicky roast lamb, then have it and love it. But at the end of the day (as they say) the bottom line (as they say) is how you *feel*: and if eating vegetarian dishes makes you feel lighter, healthier and happier with yourself, then go for it. Once you've got the hang of substituting items like pasta and vegetables, rice and lentils, on a couple of nights a week, you'll find that the whole concept really is no more trouble than fathoming the workings of a new washing machine. And the rewards are all on line: you should feel and look much better — and if you're looking and feeling good anyway, be prepared for a quantum leap.

I have made a point of using ingredients that are readily available. There's nothing exotic or wildly expensive in any of the dishes. The vegetables are all familiar; the pulses and grains are available at either supermarkets or wholefood shops; the spices can be found at supermarkets or speciality shops. And although some of the dishes do need advance planning and time in the kitchen, there are many which are really quick and easy.

Starting to include wholefoods in your diet could be a turning point. Do try. There's a whole new world of healthy ingredients and flavours just waiting to be enjoyed.

*Lynn Bedford Hall*

# SALADS &
# EGG DISHES

## BEAN SLAW

*A simple salad, and an excellent way of subtly enhancing shredded cabbage with beans for a wholesome, unpretentious summer lunch. Add a loaf of wholewheat bread and you have a nourishing and low-cost meal. I usually mix haricot and soya beans in equal quantities, but feel free to adjust according to personal preference.*

325 g (12 oz) cooked beans of choice
275 g (10 oz) carrots, coarsely grated
8 slim spring onions, chopped
2 dessert apples, peeled, diced and
tossed in lemon juice
325 g (12 oz) coarsely shredded cabbage
175 g (6 oz) raisins or sultanas, briefly
plumped in hot water and drained
herb or sea salt to taste
walnuts or toasted sunflower seeds

DRESSING
250 ml (8 fl oz) mayonnaise
250 ml (8 fl oz) soured cream or
Bulgarian yoghurt or half-and-half
15-20 ml (3-4 tsp) prepared mustard

Mix all salad ingredients, except walnuts or sunflower seeds, in large bowl. Stir ingredients for dressing until well mixed. Fold dressing into salad ingredients, cover and chill. Just before serving, mix in walnuts or sunflower seeds.
*Serves 8.*

*Mediterranean Pasta Salad (p. 18).*

# HARICOT BEAN SALAD (1)

*Also known as Flageolets Vinaigrette, this happy combination of French and Greek flavours is an economical, substantial salad to serve with wholewheat bread as a complete meal.*
*Serve with Tzatziki (p. 76).*

500 g (18 oz) haricot beans
2 bouquets garnis
2 bay leaves
5 ml (1 tsp) sea salt
3-4 leeks, thinly sliced
1 green or red pepper, seeded
and chopped
1 large stick celery, sliced
100 ml (7 tbsp) chopped parsley
a large pinch of sugar
tomato, black olives and feta cheese
for garnish

DRESSING
100 ml (7 tbsp) sunflower oil
45 ml (3 tbsp) olive oil
1 clove garlic, crushed
25 ml (5 tsp) lemon juice
2.5 ml (½ tsp) sea salt
5 ml (1 tsp) dried oregano

Soak beans in cold water overnight. The next day, drain and rinse the beans, cover them with fresh water, add bouquets garnis and bay leaves, and boil until soft, adding the salt towards the end of cooking period.

Mix all ingredients for dressing, then leave to stand while the beans are cooking.

Drain cooked beans, and spoon into a large bowl. Toss, while hot, with dressing, using a fork and taking care not to mash the beans. Add leeks, pepper, celery, parsley and sugar. Cover and stand for at least 2 hours, or chill overnight.

To serve, adjust seasoning, then spoon on to a large serving platter. Surround with chunks of tomato and top with olives. Sprinkle generously with crumbled feta.
*Serves 8.*

---

## BOUQUETS GARNIS

• 

It is possible to buy these, but if you wish to make your own from the herbs in your garden, tie together a few stalks of parsley, a bay leaf and a sprig or two of thyme. They may also be tied up in a small square of muslin.

---

## PEPPERS

• 

Red and yellow peppers are nice and mild, but green peppers have a strong flavour, when served raw, that will dominate any salad.

A real cop-out salad served by some restaurants consists of raw green peppers and onions (another pungent vegetable when served raw), tossed with lettuce and tomatoes, and doused with a vinegary dressing.

To tone down the strong flavour of raw green peppers and raw onions in a salad, blanch them. They still look attractive and should retain their crunch, but the boiling water removes the bite. Place the rings in a bowl, add a pinch of sugar, pour boiling water over them to cover, leave them in the water for a few minutes, then drain them thoroughly.

---

# AÏGROISSADE WITH AÏOLI-YOGHURT DRESSING

*A fancy name for a very simple, chunky salad of Provençal origin, combining steamed vegetables, chickpeas and a garlic dressing. This is my version, using vegetables which are available throughout the year. Serve with hot wholewheat rolls and, if liked, a bowl of grated cheese for sprinkling. It is important either to steam the vegetables, or to cook them in the very minimum amount of water, adding them in relays, as described. For this method, you'll need a wide, deep saucepan or a frying pan with a lid.*

2 leeks, sliced
2 medium potatoes, scrubbed and cut
into eighths
250 g (9 oz) slim green beans, trimmed
and sliced
3-4 carrots, julienned
250 g (9 oz) broccoli, most of stalks
discarded and coarsely chopped
325 g (12 oz) cooked chickpeas
60 g (2 oz) bean or other sprouts
100 ml (7 tbsp) finely chopped parsley
5 ml (1 tsp) sea salt and milled black
pepper to taste

DRESSING
250 ml (8 fl oz) mayonnaise
250 ml (8 fl oz) Bulgarian yoghurt
2 cloves garlic, crushed

Heat a small quantity of water in a pan and add leeks and potatoes. Cover and steam over low heat for about 7 minutes. Top with the beans, carrots and broccoli. Cover and steam for another 12-15 minutes. Test potatoes with tip of a knife and, if tender, the dish is done.

Tip the cooked vegetables into a bowl (if correctly cooked, no draining should be necessary). Add the chickpeas, chosen sprouts, parsley and seasoning. Set aside to cook while making dressing.

Stir together the mayonnaise, yoghurt and crushed garlic. Gently fold half the mixture into the vegetables. If not serving immediately, cover the salad and refrigerate until needed.

To serve, mound on to a large salad platter. Serve the remaining garlic dressing separately.
*Serves 6.*

---

## BLENDER AÏOLI

• 

Crudités, being fresh and raw, are the appropriate snack to serve with drinks before a vegetarian meal. Choose from a variety of fresh, very young vegetables: thinly sliced baby carrots, sliced sticks of celery, raw cauliflower florets, button mushrooms on cocktail sticks, fingers of cucumber and baby marrows. Arrange them in bright little piles with a bowl of boldly flavoured mayonnaise in the middle.

This mayonnaise is thick and garlicky. For a milder variation, use only 2 cloves garlic and add 5 ml (1 tsp) Dijon mustard and a generous 2.5 ml (½ tsp) dried dill before adding the oil.

4 cloves garlic
2.5 ml (½ tsp) sea salt
1 whole egg and 1 egg yolk
25 ml (5 tsp) lemon juice
125 ml (4 fl oz) each sunflower
and olive oil

Place garlic, salt, egg and yolk and lemon juice in a blender and blend until well combined. With blender running, add the oils in a slow, thin stream through the hole in the top. Stop when mixture has formed a thick emulsion. Spoon into a bowl, cover, and chill to mellow the flavour.
*Makes about 275 ml (9 fl oz).*

# CREAMY CURRIED SOYA BEAN SALAD

*This salad is sheer goodness, cheap, easy to make and much tastier than it sounds. Serve it with bowls of chutney, coconut for sprinkling, lettuce and tomato, and introduce a grain by packing a rice salad into ramekins and turning out.*

**600 g (21 oz) cooked soya beans (or half soya and half haricot)**
**1 small pineapple, cut into small dice**
**1 bunch spring onions, chopped**
**75 g (2½ oz) seedless raisins**
**2 Golden Delicious apples, peeled, diced, and tossed in lemon juice**
**onion salt or sea salt to taste**
**125 g (4 oz) coarsely chopped walnuts**

DRESSING
**20 ml (4 tsp) curry powder**
**200 ml (7 fl oz) thick mayonnaise**
**200 ml (7 fl oz) Bulgarian yoghurt**
**a pinch of sugar**

Mix all salad ingredients together except chopped walnuts.

Make the dressing by steeping the curry powder in 45 ml (3 tbsp) boiling water for a few minutes to remove the raw taste. Stir the mayonnaise with the yoghurt until smooth, then add the curry powder and a pinch of sugar. Stir to mix.

Fold dressing into salad, and chill for several hours. Toss in the walnuts just before serving.
*Serves 8.*

# RICE, CHICKPEA AND FETA SALAD

*Serve this salad with Tzatziki (p. 76) and Greek Garlic Bread (p. 94).*

DRESSING
**60 ml (4 tbsp) each sunflower and olive oil**
**45 ml (3 tbsp) lemon juice**
**30 ml (2 tbsp) finely chopped fresh marjoram leaves**
**2.5 ml (½ tsp) sea salt**
**2.5 ml (½ tsp) mustard powder**
**a pinch of sugar**

**125 g (4 oz) brown rice**
**325 g (12 oz) cooked chickpeas**
**45 ml (3 tbsp) finely chopped parsley**
**4 spring onions, chopped**
**2-3 baby marrows, pared and coarsely grated**
**90 g (3 oz) shredded spinach**
**sea salt and milled black pepper to taste**
**1 large tomato, chopped**
**crumbled feta cheese and toasted sesame seeds for garnish**

Whisk together ingredients for dressing, then cover and stand for about 1 hour.

Meanwhile, boil rice in 325 ml (11 fl oz) salted water. When ready, tip into bowl and fork in dressing while rice is hot. Add chickpeas, parsley, onions, marrows and spinach. Season very lightly, then cover and stand at room temperature to cool. Just before serving, add tomato. Pile on to serving platter and top with feta and sesame seeds.
*Serves 4.*

# CHICKPEA, RICE AND LENTIL SPROUT SALAD

*Top this bright and crunchy salad with crumbled feta cheese and/or wedges of hard-boiled eggs for added nutrition and surround with slivers of avocado and cherry tomatoes.*

**150 g (5 oz) brown rice**
**2.5 ml (½ tsp) turmeric**
**45 ml (3 tbsp) sunflower oil**
**2 large leeks, sliced**
**10 ml (2 tsp) ground coriander**
**5 ml (1 tsp) each ground cinnamon and cumin**
**550 g (19 oz) cooked chickpeas**
**15 g (½ oz) finely chopped parsley**
**90 g (3 oz) lentil sprouts**
**6 small baby marrows, pared and coarsely grated, or 125 g (4 oz) coarsely grated raw butternut squash**
**herb vegetable salt (e.g. garlic and parsley) or sea salt to taste**
**125 ml (4 fl oz) lemony French dressing**

Boil the rice in 450 ml (¾ pint) salted water with turmeric. Do not undercook — it must be quite dry and fluffy. Meanwhile, heat oil and sauté leeks until soft. Stir in spices, and toss over low heat for 1-2 minutes.

Tip cooked rice into large bowl. Fork in spicy leeks and rest of ingredients, except French dressing. Finally, toss with enough dressing to moisten thoroughly.

To serve, pile on to a platter, and garnish as suggested.
*Serves 6.*

*Overleaf: Moulded Cream Cheese and Vegetable Salad (p. 20), Piperade (p. 24) and Curried Pearled Wheat Salad (p. 12).*

# CHICKPEA SALAD WITH CABBAGE AND WALNUTS

*A creamy, crunchy salad which offers a good introduction to those unfamiliar with chickpeas. Serve mounded on a salad platter, sprinkle with the bright garnish and surround with shredded lettuce and segments of avocado. Hand a jug of French dressing and wholewheat rolls.*

550 g (19 oz) cooked chickpeas
2 Golden Delicious apples, peeled and finely diced
325 g (12 oz) shredded cabbage
1 bunch spring onions, chopped
½ pineapple, diced*
a shake of sea salt or herb salt
125 g (4 oz) coarsely chopped walnuts
finely grated Cheddar cheese for topping
finely chopped parsley for topping

DRESSING
200 ml (7 fl oz) thick mayonnaise
200 ml (7 fl oz) Bulgarian yoghurt
5 ml (1 tsp) prepared mustard
2 pinches of sugar

Toss all the salad ingredients together, except walnuts, cheese and parsley. Mix ingredients for dressing, stirring until smooth. Mix dressing with salad, then cover and chill for at least 2 hours, or overnight. Fork in nuts and sprinkle with the mixed cheese and parsley before serving.
*Serves 6–8.*

* Cut pineapple into rings and peel. Place rings flat on chopping board, slice into thin vertical strips, then cut across into tiny dice.

# BULGUR SALAD WITH RICE AND MUSHROOMS

*A delectable combination of salad ingredients, tossed with a mustard-flavoured dressing. An excellent choice for a cold buffet. Then again, with the addition of nuts or sunflower seeds, and topped with feta or grated Cheddar cheese, it makes a lovely light meal. Try it with Hummus (p. 84), tomatoes and Pitta Bread (p. 93); or simply add a creamy coleslaw.*

150 g (5 oz) bulgur
150 g (5 oz) brown rice

DRESSING
45 ml (3 tbsp) each sunflower and olive oil
45 ml (3 tbsp) lemon juice
1.25 ml (¼ tsp) sea salt
5-10 ml (1-2 tsp) prepared mustard
a pinch of sugar

30 ml (2 tbsp) sunflower oil
250 g (9 oz) brown mushrooms, wiped and sliced
2 cloves garlic, crushed
1 sprig fresh rosemary
25 ml (5 tsp) sweet sherry
1 red pepper, seeded and finely chopped
6-8 slim spring onions, chopped
100 ml (7 tbsp) finely chopped parsley
⅓ cucumber, pared and diced
sea salt and milled black pepper
chopped nuts and toasted sunflower seeds (optional)
grated cheese of choice for topping

Soak bulgur in plenty of cold water for 45 minutes. Cook rice in 450 ml (¾ pint) salted water. Whisk together ingredients for dressing and put aside.

Meanwhile, heat the 30 ml (2 tbsp) sunflower oil and add mushrooms, garlic and rosemary. Stir-fry over low heat until just softening, then add sherry and allow to evaporate. Remove pan from heat, add red pepper, cover and leave to stand.

Drain bulgur in colander and squeeze very well to release excess moisture. Spoon into large bowl and add rice, onions, parsley, cucumber and seasoning. Remove rosemary and add mushrooms to mixture, together with any juices that have formed. Fork in dressing, then cover and stand for about 2 hours for flavour to develop.

Mix in nuts or sunflower seeds, if using, and top with grated cheese.
*Serves 6.*

# CURRIED PEARLED WHOLE WHEAT SALAD

*A deliciously tangy salad in which pearled whole wheat is combined with pineapple and grated raw butternut squash in a creamy, curry dressing. The following quantities make an enormous salad which is both economical and nourishing. Serve with hard-boiled eggs and a home-made wholewheat loaf. Chopped walnuts or toasted sunflower seeds are an optional but super addition — fold them in before serving.*

300 g (11 oz) pearled whole wheat, rinsed and drained
5 ml (1 tsp) each sea salt and turmeric
2 sticks cinnamon
90 g (3 oz) seedless raisins
3 rings fresh pineapple, diced
250 g (9 oz) coarsely grated butternut squash
15 g (½ oz) finely chopped parsley
a little extra sea salt and milled black pepper to taste

DRESSING
25 ml (5 tsp) sunflower oil
3 leeks, very thinly sliced
1 red pepper, seeded and diced (optional)
15 ml (1 tbsp) curry powder
175 ml (6 fl oz) Bulgarian yoghurt
125 ml (4 fl oz) thick mayonnaise
25 ml (5 tsp) mild fruit chutney
5 ml (1 tsp) light brown sugar

Put the pearled whole wheat, 1.25 litres (2¼ pints) water, salt, turmeric and cinnamon into a saucepan. Bring to the boil, then cover and simmer for 45 minutes. Drain the cooked, pearled whole wheat, rinse, add raisins and steam in a colander, covered with a tea-towel, over simmering water for 15 minutes, or until fluffy. Remove the cinnamon sticks and spoon the rice mixture into large bowl. Fork in the pineapple, squash, parsley, and season lightly. Set the mixture aside to cool while making dressing.

Heat oil in a small pan. Add leeks, red pepper (if using) and curry powder, and stir-fry for about 2 minutes, adding a dash of water so as not to scorch the curry. Mix yoghurt, mayonnaise, chutney and sugar. Add curry mixture and stir well. Fold dressing into cooled salad, cover and refrigerate for several hours before serving.

Serve with extra chutney and a bowl of coconut, and surround the salad with sliced avocado.
*Serves 8.*

# RICE, LENTIL AND PINEAPPLE SALAD

*This salad is perfect summer fare: mound salad on a large platter, and surround it with halved hard-boiled eggs, rounded sides up and drizzled with a mustard-flavoured mayonnaise.*

200 g (7 oz) brown rice
200 g (7 oz) brown or green lentils, picked over and rinsed
125 ml (4 fl oz) sunflower oil
30 ml (2 tbsp) soy sauce
45 ml (3 tbsp) lemon juice
2.5 ml (½ tsp) ground ginger
5 ml (1 tsp) honey
½ pineapple, sliced into rings and diced
2 sticks celery, chopped
1 green or red pepper, seeded, diced and blanched
75 ml (5 tbsp) chopped parsley
90 g (3 oz) seedless raisins or sultanas, plumped in hot water and drained
2 carrots, coarsely grated
60 g (2 oz) mung beans or lentil sprouts
6 spring onions, chopped
60 g (2 oz) toasted sunflower seeds or toasted almond slivers

Cook rice in 550 ml (18 fl oz) salted water until dry and fluffy. Boil lentils in 500 ml (17 fl oz) salted water until soft and water is absorbed. Spoon rice and lentils into large bowl.

Blanch the green or red pepper in boiling water for 1 minute, then drain. Whisk together the oil, soy sauce, lemon juice, ginger and honey and fork into hot rice and lentils. Add pineapple, celery, drained pepper, parsley, raisins or sultanas, carrots, sprouts and onions. Toss well, cover and leave to cool, or chill overnight, to allow flavours to blend. Just before serving, fork in the sunflower seeds, or sprinkle toasted almond slivers over the salad.
*Serves 8–10.*

---

### BUTTERNUT SQUASH AND BEETROOT
— • —

Beetroot, especially, is a neglected vegetable because it takes time to cook. Try raw butternut squash and/or beetroot, peeled and grated in salads for extra vitamins, some bright colour and a nice crunch.

---

# RICE, LENTIL AND MUSHROOM SALAD WITH FRESH HERBS

*This is a splendid choice for a light, hot-weather lunch. It is particularly good served with butter lettuce and avocado, a bowl of Tzatziki (p. 76), hot sesame rolls and cheese. It is important to use fresh herbs in the dressing, which should be made about an hour before using to allow the full flavour to develop.*

DRESSING
100 ml (3½ fl oz) sunflower oil
25 ml (5 tsp) lemon juice
2 cloves garlic, crushed
2.5 ml (½ tsp) sea salt
25 ml (5 tsp) fresh mixed herbs, chopped*
a pinch of sugar

200 g (7 oz) brown rice
200 g (7 oz) brown or green lentils, picked over and rinsed
45 ml (3 tbsp) sunflower oil
250 g (9 oz) brown mushrooms, wiped and sliced
3 sticks celery, sliced, plus a few leaves
25 ml (5 tsp) soy sauce
100 ml (7 tbsp) finely chopped parsley
1 large onion, thinly sliced into rings
1 red pepper, seeded and diced
a pinch of sugar
toasted slivered almonds for garnish

Mix ingredients for dressing, cover and set aside for flavour to develop.

Boil rice in 550 ml (18 fl oz) salted water until fluffy and dry. Boil lentils in 500 ml (17 fl oz) salted water until soft and water is absorbed.

Meanwhile, heat oil and sauté mushrooms and celery until softening. Remove from heat and add soy sauce and parsley.

Tip the hot rice and lentils into bowl and fork in the dressing. Add the celery and mushroom mixture, plus any juices that have formed.

Pour boiling water over onion rings and diced red pepper, add a pinch of sugar and leave to stand for a few minutes. Drain and fork into salad, taking care not to mash the lentils or break up the onion rings. Cover and leave to cool.

Serve at room temperature, sprinkled with the almonds.
*Serves 6.*

* Choose from parsley, chives, basil, tarragon or marjoram.

---

# LENTIL SALAD

*This is a favourite summer lunch salad. Surround with wedges of hard-boiled eggs and serve with cheese and wholewheat bread for a nourishing, complete meal. Brighten up the lentils by drizzling a little plain yoghurt or soured cream over them and topping the salad with fresh chopped mint or a sprinkling of nuts of your choice.*

300 g (11 oz) brown lentils, picked over and rinsed
2.5 ml (½ tsp) sea salt
2 bay leaves
2.5 ml (½ tsp) turmeric
100 ml (7 tbsp) French dressing
3-4 spring onions, chopped
2 large carrots, grated
2-3 sticks celery, chopped
45 ml (3 tbsp) chopped parsley
60 g (2 oz) mung bean sprouts
25 ml (5 tsp) soy sauce

Put the lentils into a saucepan with 750 ml (1¼ pints) water, salt, bay leaves and turmeric. Bring to the boil, then cover and simmer gently until soft and liquid has been absorbed.

Tip the cooked lentils into a large bowl and discard the bay leaves. Fork in the French dressing, taking care not to mash the lentils. Add the spring onions, carrots, celery, parsley, bean sprouts and soy sauce. Toss lightly to mix, and then set aside, covered, for about 2 hours for flavours to develop, or chill for longer.

Serve as suggested.
*Serves 6.*

---

### SUGAR
— • —

I often use a little sugar in savoury dishes. It brings out the flavour, and helps to cut the acidity of ingredients such as tomatoes and buttermilk. If using white sugar, use less; if using soft, dark brown sugar, remember that it has a rather distinctive flavour.

---

*Overleaf: Spicy Indian-Style Salad (p. 21), Green Pasta Salad with Herb Dressing (p. 17) and Coronation Egg Salad (p. 24).*

## TWO-GRAIN SALAD WITH MUSHROOMS AND BABY MARROWS

*Pearled whole wheat has a lovely nutty texture and flavour and adds a new dimension to this rice and vegetable salad, which is subtly flavoured with sesame oil. The salad may be served very simply, with lettuce and a bowl of thick yoghurt, or accompanied with halved hard-boiled eggs in a lemony mayonnaise for a more substantial meal.*

150 g (5 oz) pearled whole wheat, well rinsed
200 g (7 oz) brown rice
25 ml (5 tsp) each sunflower and dark sesame oil
250 g (9 oz) brown mushrooms, wiped and sliced
1 large sprig fresh rosemary
6 spring onions, chopped
6 baby marrows, pared and very thinly sliced
100 ml (7 tbsp) finely chopped parsley
60 g (2 oz) toasted sunflower seeds or 100 g (3½ oz) toasted almond strips

DRESSING
100 ml (7 tbsp) sunflower oil
25 ml (5 tsp) soy sauce
25 ml (5 tsp) lemon juice

Cook pearled whole wheat in 800 ml (27 fl oz) salted water in a covered saucepan on low heat until soft and most of liquid has been absorbed — for about 45 minutes. Rinse the cooked pearled whole wheat in colander, then steam over boiling water until dry and fluffy.

Cook brown rice in 500 ml (18 fl oz) salted water until tender. While rice is cooking, mix ingredients for dressing. When rice is cooked, tip the hot grains into a large bowl and fork in the dressing.

Heat sunflower and sesame oils, add mushrooms and rosemary and stir-fry over medium heat until browned and beginning to soften. Remove the rosemary and add mushrooms to grains. Add remaining ingredients, toss gently, check seasoning, then cover and stand for at least 1 hour.

Mound on to a large salad platter, and serve as suggested.
*Serves 8.*

---

**MARINATED MUSHROOMS WITH LENTIL SPROUTS**

•

The easiest way to marinate mushrooms is simply to slice them, toss them with a well-flavoured vinaigrette dressing, and then leave them in the refrigerator for a couple of hours or overnight. The following recipe, not quite as simple, is more of a deliciously light and crunchy salad.

45 ml (3 tbsp) olive or sunflower oil
15 g (½ oz) butter
500 g (18 oz) white mushrooms, wiped and sliced, and halved (unless very small)
2 leeks, finely shredded
25 ml (5 tsp) soy sauce
30 ml (2 tbsp) sweet sherry
25 ml (5 tsp) toasted sesame seeds
25 ml (5 tsp) extra olive or sunflower oil
125 g (4 oz) lentil sprouts

Heat oil and butter in a large frying pan. Add mushrooms, and toss over medium heat until just beginning to brown and shrink. Do not overcook. Transfer mushrooms to a shallow salad bowl and carefully mix in leeks.

Mix together soy sauce, sherry, sesame seeds and extra oil for dressing, and add to mushrooms. Cover and refrigerate for several hours or overnight. Add lentil sprouts just before serving, mixing in lightly.
*Serves 6.*

---

## RICE AND LENTIL SPROUT SALAD

*A wonderfully nutritious combination of ingredients goes into this super salad: brown rice, lentil sprouts, fresh pineapple, baby marrows or butternut, and sunflower seeds, all tossed together with a richly flavoured, unusual dressing. This is a good buffet salad, or serve it for lunch with halved hard-boiled eggs tucked into a mustard mayonnaise or simply with crusty rolls and chunky cottage cheese. Garnish with red lettuce, chopped parsley, chives and/or bright nasturtium flowers for colour. For special occasions, add a bowl of marinated mushrooms.*

DRESSING*
125 ml (4 fl oz) sunflower oil
30 ml (2 tbsp) dark sesame oil**
30 ml (2 tbsp) soy sauce
45 ml (3 tbsp) toasted sesame seeds
45 ml (3 tbsp) lemon juice
20 ml (4 tsp) light brown sugar

300 g (11 oz) brown rice
225 g (8 oz) lentil sprouts
8 small baby marrows, pared and coarsely grated, or 250 g (9 oz) coarsely grated butternut squash
6-8 spring onions, chopped
4 thin rings fresh pineapple, diced
100 g (3½ oz) toasted sunflower seeds

Using a fork, whisk together all the ingredients for the dressing, cover and leave it to stand.

Cook rice in 850 ml (29 fl oz) lightly salted water. When done, drain (if necessary) and tip the hot rice into a large bowl. Fork in the dressing until rice is well moistened, then gently mix in the marrows or squash, onions, pineapple and sunflower seeds. Cover and leave to stand at room temperature for about 2 hours, or cover and chill until needed, but return to room temperature before serving.

Spoon on to a salad platter, and garnish as suggested.
*Serves 8.*

* To add a lovely flavour to a tossed green salad, combine this dressing with basic French dressing, using a ratio of 1:2.

** If using a light sesame oil, use about 45 ml (3 tbsp) and decrease the amount of sunflower oil accordingly.

# SESAME RICE SALAD

*A delectable combination of rice, mushrooms, cucumber and seeds, this salad has an Oriental touch. Serve as part of a cold buffet, or as a wholesome, light meal, with the addition of stuffed hard-boiled eggs and wholewheat bread.*

**150 g (5 oz) brown rice**
**150 g (5 oz) brown lentils, picked over and rinsed**
**60 ml (4 tbsp) sunflower oil**
**2 leeks, sliced, or 1 large onion, finely chopped**
**1 red pepper, seeded and diced**
**250 g (9 oz) brown mushrooms, wiped and sliced**
**½ cucumber, pared and julienned**
**2 sprigs fresh rosemary**
**100 ml (7 tbsp) chopped parsley**
**100 ml (7 tbsp) toasted sunflower seeds**
**30 ml (2 tbsp) toasted sesame seeds**
**bean or other sprouts for garnish**

### DRESSING
**45 ml (3 tbsp) soy sauce**
**25 ml (5 tsp) sweet sherry**
**5 ml (1 tsp) light brown sugar**
**15 ml (1 tbsp) dark sesame oil**

Boil rice in 450 ml (¾ pint) lightly salted water and lentils in 400 ml (14 fl oz) lightly salted water. Keep the heat low, the saucepans covered, and avoid stirring and looking. They should be cooked in 50 minutes.

Meanwhile, heat the sunflower oil and stir-fry the leeks or onion and red pepper. When softening, add mushrooms, cucumber and rosemary and toss over low heat until just tender. Remove from heat, remove rosemary, mix in parsley and seeds and set aside.

Mix ingredients for dressing. Drain cooked rice and lentils, if necessary, and tip into large bowl. Fork in mushroom mixture, adding all the juices. Toss with dressing. Cool, then cover loosely and stand for 1-2 hours. Serve garnished with bean sprouts.
*Serves 6.*

# BULGUR SALAD WITH TOMATOES AND BLACK OLIVES

*Bulgur wheat, used extensively in the Middle East, is sold at some health-food shops. The grains are soaked, then toasted, after which they need only be soaked in water. Cracked wheat cannot be substituted. This delicious and unusual salad can be served as a light main course with Hummus (p. 84) and Pitta Bread (p. 93).*

### DRESSING
**45 ml (3 tbsp) each sunflower and olive oil**
**30 ml (2 tbsp) lemon juice**
**1 clove garlic, crushed**
**sea salt and milled black pepper to taste**
**2.5 ml (½ tsp) dried oregano**

**250 g (9 oz) bulgur**
**6 small spring onions, finely chopped**
**100 ml (7 tbsp) finely chopped parsley**
**25 ml (5 tsp) finely chopped fresh mint**
**2 medium tomatoes, chopped**
**black olives, sliced**
**lettuce and sliced cucumber for garnish**

Mix ingredients for dressing first, and stand for several hours to blend flavours.

Cover bulgur generously with water and soak for about 45 minutes. Drain in colander and squeeze out excess moisture with hands. Put into large bowl and add onions, parsley and mint. Pour prepared dressing over bulgur, toss, cover and stand for 30 minutes. Adjust seasoning, then fold in tomatoes and some olives. Serve garnished with lettuce and sliced cucumber.
*Serves 6.*

# GREEN PASTA SALAD WITH HERB DRESSING

*This is a stunning salad in which pasta spirals, or fusilli noodles, are coated with a pale green sauce, subtly spiked with basil. Pretty to look at and deliciously flavoured, it is bound to find favour with those who enjoy Mediterranean-style foods. The sauce is quickly made in a blender while the pasta is cooking and the dish is then chilled for several hours, making it a perfect choice for a do-ahead summer supper or buffet. It is not, however, a dish that can stand alone, but it does make a beautiful accompaniment to chickpea or bean salads; or for a light meal simply add a well-dressed spinach salad with croûtons, mushrooms and hard-boiled eggs.*

**250 g (9 oz) pasta spirals, fusilli noodles or elbow macaroni**
**15 g (½ oz) parsley sprigs**
**20 g (¾ oz) shredded fresh basil leaves**
**1 small clove garlic**
**2 spring onions, chopped**
**125 ml (4 fl oz) thick mayonnaise**
**125 ml (4 fl oz) buttermilk**
**45 ml (3 tbsp) olive oil**
**2.5 ml (½ tsp) sea salt and a pinch of sugar**
**extra olive oil or a little French dressing**
**chopped walnuts (optional)**
**black olives and feta or Parmesan cheese for garnish**

Cook chosen pasta in plenty of rapidly boiling salted water, drain, toss with a dash of oil, and leave to cool.

Put parsley, basil, garlic, onions, mayonnaise, buttermilk, oil, salt and sugar into a blender and blend well to a medium-thick mixture, flecked with green.*

Tip pasta into a large bowl, mix in sauce, cover and chill.

Before serving, gently fork in a little olive oil or French dressing to add shine and loosen the pasta. Check seasoning (it will probably need a little salt), add walnuts if using, pile on to large serving platter, tuck in some olives and top with either crumbled feta or grated Parmesan. Offer a pepper mill at the table.
*Serves 4–6, depending on the rest of the meal.*

* The longer you blend the sauce, the brighter the colour will be. A very well blended sauce should be a bright peppermint green colour.

# MEDITERRANEAN PASTA SALAD

*This jumbo salad is known in our house as El Cheapo, but the economy of the salad in no way detracts from its appeal. Visually it's quite beautiful: fusilli noodles tossed with vegetables in all the bright colours. A hot crusty loaf is an essential accompaniment.*

250 g (9 oz) fusilli noodles
30 ml (2 tbsp) each sunflower
and olive oil
1 onion, chopped
2 large leeks, sliced
2 cloves garlic, crushed
1 red pepper, seeded and diced
5 ml (1 tsp) dried oregano
2.5 ml (½ tsp) dried thyme
500 g (18 oz) aubergines, cubed
and dégorged
45 ml (3 tbsp) each water and white wine
3-4 carrots, julienned
2 sticks celery, sliced
325 g (12 oz) baby marrows, pared and
thinly sliced
100 ml (7 tbsp) chopped parsley
sea salt and milled black pepper to taste
2-3 tomatoes, chopped
25 ml (5 tsp) French dressing
a pinch of sugar
feta or Cheddar cheese and a few
black olives for garnish

Cook noodles in plenty of salted water, drain well, toss with a dash of oil and place in a large bowl.

Heat the oils in a large pan, add the onion, leeks, garlic, red pepper and herbs. Sauté for a few minutes, while you sniff the marvellous aroma released by the herbs. Add the aubergines, water and wine, then cover the pan and simmer for about 10 minutes, until the aubergines are cooked.

Mix in carrots, celery, baby marrows, parsley and seasoning, then cover and simmer for 5-6 minutes until vegetables are just tender. Do not overcook. Pour the vegetable mixture over the noodles, carefully fork in the tomatoes and dressing, and add a pinch of sugar to bring out the flavour. Cover the salad loosely and stand for about 2 hours to mellow flavour, or refrigerate overnight.

Spoon on to large salad platter. Top with plenty of crumbled feta or grated Cheddar cheese and stud with a few olives.
*Serves 8–10.*

# CREAMY PASTA, CHEESE AND PINEAPPLE SALAD

*An interesting combination of ingredients goes into this delicious salad. The list may be long, but the ingredients are all easily obtainable and the salad itself is a breeze to put together. It may be chilled overnight but should be served at room temperature. Surround with red lettuce leaves and garnish with sliced avocado.*

250 g (9 oz) elbow macaroni
25 ml (5 tsp) each sunflower
and sesame oil
2 red or yellow peppers (or one of each),
seeded and diced
2 sticks celery, plus a few leaves, sliced
250 g (9 oz) white button mushrooms,
halved or left whole
sea salt and milled black pepper to taste
425 g (15 oz) canned pineapple rings
in natural juice, drained and diced
(reserve juice)
6 spring onions, chopped
275 g (10 oz) shredded cabbage
2 large carrots, coarsely grated
200 g (7 oz) cheese (preferably low-fat
Edam), cut into small cubes
100 g (3½ oz) coarsely chopped walnuts
or
60 g (2 oz) toasted sunflower seeds
45 ml (3 tbsp) mayonnaise

DRESSING
100 ml (7 tbsp) sunflower oil
100 ml (7 tbsp) drained pineapple juice
45 ml (3 tbsp) soy sauce
a big pinch of sugar

Cook pasta in lots of salted water with a dash of oil. Drain thoroughly.

Heat sunflower and sesame oils and stir-fry peppers and celery until tender-crisp. Add mushrooms and toss over medium heat until softening but still chunky — do not overcook. Remove from heat, season and tip into a large bowl with the drained pasta. Add the pineapple, onions, cabbage and carrots.

Mix ingredients for dressing and pour over salad. Toss well, and then mix in cubed cheese and walnuts or sunflower seeds. Cover the salad and cool for at least an hour, or chill overnight (but return to room temperature before serving).

Just before serving, fold in mayonnaise and serve as suggested.
*Serves 8.*

# PASTA AND BUTTER BEAN SALAD

*Plain and spinach fusilli noodles, creamy butter beans, a stir-fry of bright vegetables — this is such a pretty salad, and so easy to make. The cheese and sunflower seeds add nutrition, and with the addition of a hot herb loaf it makes a super summer meal. Keep it simple, or add fresh salad leaves, baby tomatoes, small spears of corn and/or segments of avocado for a colourful garnish.*

175 g (6 oz) each plain and spinach
fusilli noodles*
45 ml (3 tbsp) sunflower oil
30 ml (2 tbsp) olive oil
1 bunch spring onions, chopped
1 leek, sliced
2 cloves garlic, crushed
1 green or red pepper, seeded and diced
4 medium carrots, julienned
2.5 ml (½ tsp) each dried oregano
and basil
90 g (3 oz) shredded spinach
125-250 g (4-9 oz) button mushrooms,
wiped and halved
25 ml (5 tsp) sweet sherry
400 g (14 oz) canned choice grade butter
beans, drained
5 ml (1 tsp) sea salt and milled black
pepper to taste
125 g (4 oz) finely grated low-fat
cheese (such as Edam)
60 g (2 oz) toasted sunflower seeds
(optional)

Boil fusilli noodles in plenty of salted water with a dash of oil.

Meanwhile, heat both oils in a large pan. Add onions, leek, garlic, diced pepper, carrots and herbs and stir-fry over medium heat. When softening, add spinach, mushrooms and sherry and toss together until spinach wilts and sherry has evaporated.

Drain pasta and tip into a large bowl. Add beans and fork in vegetable mixture. Season and set aside to cool. Fork in cheese and sunflower seeds, if using, when cold.

Serve this salad at room temperature.
*Serves 6.*

* Or use only one kind if preferred, but the salad won't be as cheerful.

*Bulgur, Chickpea and Spinach Salad (p. 25) and Two-Bean Fruit and Nut Salad in Lemon Mayonnaise (p. 21).*

# MOULDED CREAM CHEESE AND VEGETABLE SALAD

*A super crunchy luncheon salad in which steamed vegetables are folded into a creamy mixture, chilled until set and then turned out. Surround with bright salad leaves and serve with a rice and mushroom salad.*

500 g (18 oz) mixed fresh vegetables*
5 ml (1 tsp) each sea salt and
dried tarragon
250 g (9 oz) cream cheese
125 ml (4 fl oz) soured cream
125 ml (4 fl oz) mayonnaise
10 ml (2 tsp) Dijon mustard
60 g (2 oz) bean or other sprouts**
45 ml (3 tbsp) finely chopped parsley
20 ml (4 tsp) powdered gelatine
2 egg whites, whisked
milled black pepper

Steam the prepared mixed vegetables in the minimum amount of salted water until just cooked. Towards end of cooking period, add the sea salt and crushed tarragon. Set aside to cool.

Stir together the cream cheese, soured cream, mayonnaise and mustard until smooth. Mix in the vegetables (drained if necessary), chosen sprouts and parsley.

Sprinkle gelatine on to 60 ml (4 tbsp) cold water in a small container and dissolve over low heat, then slowly dribble into the cheese mixture while stirring. Fold in the egg whites and pepper, and pour into a rinsed mould (capacity at least 1.5 litres/2³/₄ pints), then refrigerate until set.

Unmould and garnish as suggested. This recipe may be made a day in advance and the salad kept in the refrigerator.
*Serves 8.*

* I use a mixture of chopped broccoli, pared and sliced baby marrows, green peas, a small, diced carrot for colour and a large leek, thinly shredded. Use your own selection, if preferred, but do include a leek or a bunch of chopped spring onions.

** If liked, use a mixture; alternatively, you could add a handful of chopped walnuts, for crunch. A couple of hard-boiled eggs, sliced, may also be folded into the mixture before chilling.

# SOFT CHEESE, CUCUMBER AND PASTA MOULD

*A creamy, moulded salad. Turn out and surround with a mushroom and rice salad, segments of avocado, and cherry tomatoes to spark up the colour. Lovely for a summer lunch.*

¹/₃-²/₃ large cucumber
125 g (4 oz) elbow macaroni
250 g (9 oz) low-fat soft cheese*
100 ml (7 tbsp) thick mayonnaise
125 ml (4 fl oz) soured cream*
5 ml (1 tsp) Dijon mustard
15 ml (1 tbsp) powdered gelatine
1 bunch young spring onions, chopped
2 hard-boiled eggs, coarsely chopped
45 ml (3 tbsp) finely chopped parsley
a little sea salt, milled black pepper
2 egg whites
a pinch of sugar
walnut halves for garnish

Pare cucumber and grate coarsely into a colander. Salt lightly, weight and leave to drain. Cook the macaroni in plenty of salted water. Drain.

Use a wooden spoon to cream together soft cheese, mayonnaise, soured cream and mustard. Dissolve gelatine in 60 ml (4 tbsp) water over low heat and trickle slowly into cheese mixture, beating well. Add onions, hard-boiled eggs and parsley. Squeeze all moisture from cucumber between palms and add to the cheese and egg mixture, together with macaroni. Mix in seasoning. Whisk egg whites stiffly with pinch of sugar and fold in. Pour into rinsed mould, preferably a loaf-shaped china dish, at least 1.25-litre (2¹/₄-pint) capacity. Refrigerate until set. Run a knife round edges to unmould on to a large serving platter, garnish with walnut halves, and serve as suggested.
*Serves 6–8.*

* For a richer mould, use cream cheese instead of soft, or use 125 ml (4 fl oz) double cream, whipped, instead of the soured cream, but use one alternative, not both.

# CHILLED MUSHROOM AND CHEESE TART

*A good choice to feature on a luncheon menu or as part of a cold buffet. The crust can be omitted and the filling set in a mould and then turned out. Garnish with slices of avocado and a dusting of milled black pepper.*

CRUST
125 g (4 oz) crushed savoury biscuits
100 g (3¹/₂ oz) melted butter

FILLING
25 ml (5 tsp) sunflower oil
6 spring onions, chopped
250 g (9 oz) white button mushrooms,
wiped and sliced
1 clove garlic, crushed
2 sprigs fresh rosemary
1 red pepper, seeded and diced
1 stick celery, sliced
250 g (9 oz) low-fat soft cheese
2 eggs, separated
20 ml (4 tsp) powdered gelatine
100 ml (7 tbsp) vegetable stock or water
5 ml (1 tsp) sea salt
125 ml (4 fl oz) double cream, whipped
a few drops of Worcestershire sauce

Mix biscuits and butter and press into base of deep, greased 20-cm (8-in) pie dish. Chill.

Heat oil in large frying pan and add onions, mushrooms, garlic, rosemary, red pepper and celery. Toss over medium heat for about 3 minutes until starting to shrink and soften. Remove and set aside. So that juices are not extracted, do not season until just before adding to cheese mixture.

Beat cheese and yolks together until smooth. Sprinkle gelatine on to stock or water, dissolve over low heat, then slowly whisk into the cheese mixture. Remove rosemary from vegetables, add salt and mix into cheese mixture. Chill until just starting to thicken. Whisk egg whites with pinch of salt and fold in, with cream and Worcestershire sauce. Pour on to crust, or into mould, and chill until set. Garnish as suggested.
*Serves 6–8.*

---

To transform old-fashioned cabbage salad into something really special, toss it with pesto-flavoured mayonnaise. Mix thick Bulgarian yoghurt until smooth, and stir in pesto (p. 28) to taste.

Fold into shredded cabbage, together with grated carrots and any other salad ingredient of your choice; bean or other sprouts are a good addition, as well as sunflower seeds or shredded spinach.

## QUICK HOME-MADE MAYONNAISE

·

Made in a blender, this is a thick, rich mayonnaise, whipped up in minutes. Flavour, if you like, with fresh herbs, chilli sauce or green peppercorns. For a lighter mayonnaise, fold in buttermilk or Bulgarian yoghurt.

**2 whole eggs and 2 yolks**
**5 ml (1 tsp) sea salt**
**5 ml (1 tsp) mustard powder**
**60 ml (4 tbsp) lemon juice**
**500 ml (17 fl oz) sunflower oil**
**5 ml (1 tsp) light brown sugar**
**1-2 cloves garlic, chopped**

Put eggs and yolks, salt, mustard, lemon juice, 45 ml (3 tbsp) of the oil, the sugar and garlic into blender goblet and process until well mixed. With motor running, slowly drizzle in remaining oil through the hole in the lid. When all the oil has been added, you should have a smooth, thick mixture. Store in a glass jar in the refrigerator.
*Makes about 600 ml (1 pint).*

## RICE AND PECAN NUT SALAD

*A basic recipe for a simple rice salad, using the minimum of ingredients. It is very good as it stands, but try baby marrows instead of the carrots, sunflower seeds instead of the pecan nuts, while sliced sautéed mushrooms will give it a special lift.*

**300 g (11 oz) brown rice**
**100 ml (7 tbsp) herb French dressing**
**100 ml (7 tbsp) finely chopped parsley**
**6 spring onions, chopped**
**1–2 sticks celery, sliced**
**2 carrots, coarsely grated**
**100 g (3½ oz) chopped, toasted pecan nuts**
**15 ml (1 tbsp) soy sauce**

Boil rice in 800 ml (27 fl oz) water with 2.5 ml (½ tsp) salt. When cooked and all water has been absorbed, tip into a large bowl and fork in the dressing. Add remaining ingredients, tossing gently to mix, then cover and stand at room temperature for about 1 hour.
*Serves 8.*

## TWO-BEAN FRUIT AND NUT SALAD IN LEMON MAYONNAISE

*Chock-full of protein (from the beans and nuts) and vitamins (from the fruit), this salad will appeal to those who are interested in new ways of serving health foods. The beans are covertly tucked into a combination of fresh ingredients, and the result is rather like a main-course fruit salad. A good choice for a vegetarian summer lunch, served with scoops of chunky cottage cheese nestled in fresh lettuce leaves and a crunchy wholewheat loaf.*

**300 g (11 oz) cooked soya beans**
**300 g (11 oz) cooked haricot beans**
**2 Golden Delicious apples, peeled, diced and sprinkled with lemon juice**
**3-4 rings fresh pineapple, diced or**
**2 firm bananas, thinly sliced and sprinkled with lemon juice**
**125 g (4 oz) coarsely chopped walnuts**
**2 large carrots, coarsely grated**
**6 spring onions, chopped**
**90 g (3 oz) seedless raisins, plumped in hot water and drained**
**2.5 ml (½ tsp) sea salt**

DRESSING
**175 ml (6 fl oz) Bulgarian yoghurt**
**200 ml (7 fl oz) thick mayonnaise**
**10 ml (2 tsp) clear honey**
**5 ml (1 tsp) finely grated lemon rind**

Mix all the salad ingredients together in a large bowl. Stir the ingredients for the dressing together until smooth. Fold the prepared dressing into the salad until well combined, and then cover and chill for 2-3 hours or overnight for flavour to develop. Toss the salad again just before serving.
*Serves 6–8.*

## HERBS AND SPICES

·

These are extensively used in vegetarian cooking, which otherwise runs the risk of being rather bland. When bought in packets, they should be transferred to glass jars and kept tightly closed, as the flavours diminish quite quickly, and certain varieties, like sage and cumin, become musty.

## SPICY INDIAN-STYLE SALAD

*A bright and flavourful mix of rice, lentils and vegetables which will team up well with any bean or chickpea salad. Looks great on a cold buffet or may be served as a complete meal, topped with strips of cold omelette and accompanied with a bowl of mint-flavoured yoghurt. Toasted almonds are an optional but excellent addition.*

**100 g (3½ oz) brown rice**
**100 g (3½ oz) brown lentils, picked over and rinsed**
**10 ml (2 tsp) sea salt**
**3 star anise**
**2.5 ml (½ tsp) turmeric**
**6 white cardamom pods**
**2 bay leaves**
**2.5 ml (½ tsp) ground cinnamon**
**75 ml (2½ fl oz) sunflower oil**
**10 ml (2 tsp) lemon juice**
**2 medium onions, sliced into thin rings**
**2 cloves garlic, crushed**
**1 red pepper, seeded and diced**
**10 ml (2 tsp) each masala for vegetables and ground coriander**
**4 carrots, julienned**
**250 g (9 oz) broccoli sprigs**
**150 g (5 oz) green peas, fresh or frozen**

Put rice, lentils, 550 ml (18 fl oz) water, 5 ml (1 tsp) of the salt, anise, turmeric, cardamom, bay leaves and cinnamon in a saucepan, stir to mix, bring to the boil, then cover and simmer on very low heat for 50-60 minutes. While rice is cooking, prepare vegetables.

Remove spices from the rice and then tip rice into a large bowl. Mix 30 ml (2 tbsp) of the sunflower oil with the lemon juice and fork through the rice mixture.

Heat the remaining oil in a large frying pan and soften onions, garlic and red pepper. Add masala and coriander and sizzle for 1-2 minutes. Add vegetables, toss to coat with spices, then add the remaining salt and a splash of water. Cook, half-covered, until vegetables are just tender, then add to rice mixture, tossing with two forks to combine. Cover, and set aside to cool or chill overnight.

Garnish as suggested.
*Serves 4–6.*

*Overleaf: Pasta and Butter Bean Salad (p. 18), Chickpea Salad with Cabbage and Walnuts (p. 12) and Aïgroissade with Aïoli-Yoghurt Dressing (p. 8).*

# CORONATION EGG SALAD

*Based on the popular recipe for Coronation Chicken, this dish features hard-boiled eggs smothered in a creamy, spicy sauce. It is a perfect choice for an elegant, light luncheon, served with a rice salad and bowls of chutney, coconut, sliced bananas, and chopped tomato with spring onions.*

**12 eggs (hard-boiled and sliced
in half lengthways)
15 ml (1 tbsp) sunflower oil
1 large onion, finely chopped
5 ml (1 tsp) each curry powder, ground
coriander, cumin and fennel
2.5 ml (½ tsp) turmeric
10 ml (2 tsp) tomato purée
100 ml (7 tbsp) each red wine and water
1 bay leaf
15 ml (1 tbsp) smooth apricot jam
200 ml (7 fl oz) thick mayonnaise
200 ml (7 fl oz) buttermilk
paprika and toasted almonds (optional)
for garnish**

While eggs are boiling, heat oil in a small saucepan, add onion and cook gently until just softening — do not brown. Add all the spices and toss to mix, then add just a dash of water to prevent scorching and cook over very low heat for a minute or two. Add tomato purée, wine, water, bay leaf and jam. Stir to mix, then simmer, uncovered, for about 10 minutes until reduced and thickened. Strain mixture and discard onions. You should have just over 100 ml (7 tbsp) of richly coloured sauce. Allow to cool, then slowly stir into mayonnaise. When combined, slowly stir in buttermilk.

Arrange eggs, rounded sides up, on a large serving platter. Blanket with sauce, dust eggs with paprika and scatter with almonds, if using. Chill for at least 1 hour.
*Serves 6.*

---

### CORIANDER
·

Fresh, chopped coriander may be used for sprinkling on curries, but as it has a distinctive, rather pungent flavour, it is often used simply as a garnish, like its cousin, parsley. It is obtainable from shops which sell fresh herbs.

---

### TOMATOES
·

Even when cooked for a long time, as in sauces and casseroles, fresh tomatoes always have the best flavour. However, cans are convenient, but choice grade should always be used. Brands differ with regard to the number and size of tomatoes, and the amount of juice, so be prepared to adjust how much you use so that sauces do not end up too thick or too watery.

To skin fresh tomatoes, pour boiling water over, stand for a few minutes, then run under cold water. Nick out stem ends, and then slip off the skins.

---

# PIPERADE

*A Spanish dish of eggs gently scrambled in a mixture of cooked onions, peppers and tomatoes. Although this is not a main-course dish, it does make a tasty light meal and a change from plain scrambled eggs. The Basques like to eat it with their light, white Shepherd's Bread, but it is also good on wholewheat toast, or with croûtons; it may also be served cold, in hollowed out rolls, or as a stuffing for Pitta Bread (p. 93).*

**15 ml (1 tbsp) each sunflower
and olive oil
1 small red pepper, seeded and diced
1 small green pepper, seeded and diced
4 small baby marrows, pared and diced
1 medium onion, finely chopped
2 medium tomatoes, skinned
and chopped
1-2 cloves garlic, crushed
sea salt and milled black pepper to taste
a pinch of sugar
8 eggs, lightly beaten
a little finely chopped parsley and/or
fresh basil for garnish**

Heat sunflower and olive oils in a large pan and add red and green peppers, marrows and onion. Toss over low heat for about 5 minutes until softening and shrinking, then add tomatoes, garlic, seasoning and a pinch of sugar. Cover and simmer gently until the vegetables are cooked, stirring occasionally. If the tomatoes are very juicy, remove lid towards end of cooking period to drive off excess moisture. When vegetables are cooked, add eggs and stir over low heat until thick and creamy.

Turn on to warmed serving platter and sprinkle with parsley and/or basil.
*Serves 4.*

---

# CURRIED EGGS

*Eggs in a simple, tangy sauce; for best flavour, make in advance and leave to cool, then reheat. A little coconut and cream stirred in at the end are optional but delicious additions, and the coconut should also thicken the sauce to just the right consistency. Serve on brown rice, with condiments of your choice.*

**8-10 hard-boiled eggs
75 ml (5 tbsp) sunflower oil
2 onions, finely chopped
2 green or red peppers, seeded and diced
2 Golden Delicious apples, peeled
and finely diced
about 25 ml (5 tsp) curry powder
5 ml (1 tsp) turmeric
60 g (2 oz) brown flour
1.25 litres (2¼ pints) hot vegetable
stock or water
30 ml (2 tbsp) tomato purée
sea salt to taste
2 bay leaves
100 ml (7 tbsp) chutney
30 ml (2 tbsp) lemon juice
5 ml (1 tsp) dried mint
a big pinch of sugar
a little desiccated coconut (optional)
45 ml (3 tbsp) double cream (optional)**

While the eggs are boiling, make the sauce. Heat the sunflower oil in a large pan and lightly fry the onions, peppers and apples. Add the curry powder and turmeric and stir for 1 minute. Stir in the flour, then slowly add the stock or water, stirring until thickened. Add the tomato purée, sea salt, bay leaves, chutney, lemon juice, mint and sugar. Bring to the boil, then turn heat to very low and simmer the sauce, covered, for about 25 minutes, stirring occasionally. If working ahead, cool, transfer to a bowl, cover and chill until needed.

To serve, remove bay leaves and reheat (if necessary), adding the hard-boiled eggs, and coconut and cream if using.
*Serves 5–6.*

---

### BULGUR
·

This is a fibre-rich, pre-cooked, cracked wheat which needs no further cooking if the fine-grated variety is used. For salads, simply soak it for 30-45 minutes, squeeze it dry in your hands, and it is ready for use.

---

# BULGUR, CHICKPEA AND SPINACH SALAD

*A total departure from the usual bulgur, mint and parsley combination, this salad makes a splendid filling for Pitta Bread (p. 93), or serve it on a big salad platter, topped with feta and olives. Add a lettuce and bean sprout salad and include a hot crusty loaf and Garlic Butter (p. 92), or Greek Garlic Bread (p. 94).*

**150 g (5 oz) bulgur**
**150 g (5 oz) finely shredded, young
  spinach leaves, ribs removed**
**325 g (12 oz) cooked chickpeas**
**1 bunch slim spring onions, chopped**
**sea salt and milled black pepper to taste**
**25 ml (5 tsp) finely chopped fresh
  marjoram leaves**
**a handful of rocket leaves
  (if available)**
**60 g (2 oz) toasted sunflower seeds**
**2 tomatoes, chopped**
**crumbled feta cheese and olives
  for garnish**

Soak the bulgur in lots of cold water for 45 minutes. Mix all the ingredients for the dressing, cover and leave to stand for flavour to develop. Then drain bulgur in colander and squeeze very well with hands to release all moisture. Spoon into large bowl and add spinach, chickpeas, onions, seasoning and herbs. Add dressing, toss to mix thoroughly, then cover and stand for 1-2 hours or chill overnight.

Just before serving, fork in sunflower seeds and tomato. Garnish as suggested. *Serves 6.*

# SESAME NOODLE SALAD WITH TAHINI

*Unusual and delicious, this looks like a rice salad but it actually consists of tiny rice-shaped noodles, mixed with vegetables and a creamy tahini dressing. Top with rolled, thinly sliced omelette, and serve with a bean or chickpea salad for a different and delicious cold meal.*

**25 ml (5 tsp) sunflower oil**
**10 ml (2 tsp) dark sesame oil**
**2 cloves garlic, crushed**
**6-8 spring onions, chopped**
**1 red or green pepper, seeded, diced
  and thinly shredded**
**1 stick celery, sliced**
**250 g (9 oz) baby marrows, pared
  and julienned**
**1 knob root ginger, peeled and grated**
**250 g (9 oz) white mushrooms, wiped
  and thickly sliced**
**250 g (9 oz) rice-shaped noodles**
**60 g (2 oz) toasted almond strips or
  toasted cashew bits or a handful
  of toasted sesame seeds**
**3-egg omelette and bean sprouts for
  garnish (optional)**

DRESSING
**45-60 ml (3-4 tbsp) tahini**
**25 ml (5 tsp) soy sauce**
**about 30 ml (1 tbsp) water**

Heat sunflower and sesame oils and stir-fry garlic, onions, pepper, celery, baby marrows and ginger. Add mushrooms and toss over medium heat until just changing colour — they should still be firm. Do not season. Remove from heat, cover and stand while cooking noodles.

Boil the rice-shaped noodles in plenty of salted water until just *al dente* — do not overcook. Drain, rinse under cold water, and tip into a large bowl. Using a fork, carefully mix vegetable mixture into noodles.

Using the back of a spoon, cream together tahini, soy sauce and just enough water to make a mayonnaise-like mixture. This takes a few minutes, as tahini is thick.

Using a fork, toss the tahini dressing with noodle mixture, adding nuts or seeds. Check seasoning and add a little salt if necessary. Do not be tempted to add more soy sauce as you don't want too dark a colour. Cover loosely and leave to stand for about 1 hour.

Serve at room temperature, and garnish as suggested.
*Serves 6.*

# PASTA, PIZZA & QUICHES

## PASTA WITH HERBS AND EGGS

*No heavy sauces here: in this dish pasta is lightly coated with a delicately perfumed mixture of herbs and just-cooked eggs. A dish for the gourmet rather than the gourmand and a good standby when you have four people with finely attuned palates to please — in a hurry. It should be served with lots of freshly grated Parmesan and milled black pepper, a round of fluffy, crusty bread and a green salad. Home-made pasta is called for — my preference being mixed green and white fusilli noodles.*

250 g (9 oz) pasta
60 ml (4 tbsp) olive oil
15 g (½ oz) butter
1-2 cloves garlic, crushed
1 bunch slim spring onions, chopped
75 ml (5 tbsp) sunflower seeds
1.25 ml (¼ tsp) dried oregano
4-5 eggs, beaten
2.5 ml (½ tsp) sea salt
60 ml (4 tbsp) chopped fresh basil leaves
60 ml (4 tbsp) chopped parsley

Cook pasta in plenty of salted water, toss with a dash of oil and set aside.

Heat oil and butter in a large frying pan, add garlic, onions, sunflower seeds and oregano and toss over low heat until seeds are golden brown. Mix in cooked, drained pasta, and when thoroughly heated, add lightly beaten eggs with salt and herbs. Stir over lowest heat until eggs are just cooked and serve immediately.
*Makes 4 modest servings.*

*Tagliatelli with Pesto (p. 28).*

# PESTO

*Although pesto is a traditional Genoese sauce which is used to top all types of pasta and gnocchi, there are many subtle variations in the recipe. Some cooks use lashings of oil and cheese and the minimum amount of basil, others load it with garlic and some even add butter. Fortunately it's a most adaptable mixture — ripe with flavour, bright in colour and very rich. (Some people dilute it, before serving, with a little of the water in which the pasta was cooked.)*

*The first recipe contains the standard ingredients, except for pine nuts, which are by far the best to use but exorbitant in price; the second, which takes liberties with the nuts and the cheese, is my favourite — it is 'lighter', cheaper and tastes superb. However, both may be adjusted according to personal taste. Remember that pesto need not be limited to pasta. Try a teaspoonful stirred into minestrone, for instance, or serve with vegetables, tomato salad or baked potatoes instead of soured cream. However you use it, bear in mind that a little goes a long way.*

*In the case of both sauces, remove from refrigerator about 30 minutes before serving, stir to mix, and make sure that the pasta and the plates are very hot, as pesto is not heated.*

## RECIPE 1

**90 g (3 oz) fresh basil leaves,
washed and dried
30 g (1 oz) parsley sprigs
2-3 cloves garlic
12 large walnut halves
75 ml (5 tbsp) finely grated
Parmesan cheese
175 ml (6 fl oz) good quality olive oil
sea salt and milled black pepper to taste**

Place all ingredients, except oil and seasoning, in a processor fitted with the grinding blade and process until very finely chopped. With motor running, slowly dribble in the oil in a steady stream to make a thick, green purée. Add seasoning, then spoon into a jar. Run a thin film of olive oil over the top, cover and refrigerate. Pesto will keep for a couple of days and may also be frozen. Some cooks prefer to omit the Parmesan if pesto is to be frozen, adding it when the pesto is thawed and just prior to serving.

---

Always rinse feta cheese before use to remove saltiness.

---

## RECIPE 2

**2 bunches of spinach
60 g (2 oz) toasted sunflower seeds
3 cloves garlic
60 g (2 oz) fresh basil leaves,
washed and dried
125 g (4 oz) finely grated Cheddar cheese
sea salt and milled black pepper to taste
125 ml (4 fl oz) each sunflower
and olive oil**

Trim and wash spinach — you should have 500 g (18 oz) leaves, weighed after treatment. Cook until soft (the water adhering to the leaves is sufficient moisture to cook it in). Drain well, pressing out moisture with a wooden spoon.

Using a processor fitted with the grinding blade, process the sunflower seeds, garlic and basil until finely chopped. Add the cooked spinach, cheese and seasoning. Process again, and then add the oils in a thin, steady stream. The final mixture should be thick and creamy. Spoon into a jar, run a thin film of olive oil over the top, close and store in refrigerator.

# MEDITERRANEAN VEGETABLE SAUCE

*Regard this as a basic recipe as other vegetables, like mushrooms or baby marrows, may be added. Ladle it over pasta or brown rice, and top each serving with soured cream mixed with chopped chives, then sprinkle with grated cheese.*

**25 ml (5 tsp) each sunflower
and olive oil
4 large leeks, thinly sliced
3 cloves garlic, crushed
1 green pepper, seeded and diced
2 sticks celery, sliced
2 medium aubergines, rinsed,
dégorged and diced
400 g (14 oz) tomatoes, skinned
and chopped
25 ml (5 tsp) tomato purée
5 ml (1 tsp) dried basil
100 ml (7 tbsp) chopped parsley
sea salt and milled black pepper to taste
5 ml (1 tsp) sugar
125 ml (4 fl oz) vegetable stock or water
sliced black olives (optional)**

Heat oils in a very large, heavy frying pan. Add leeks and garlic. Reduce heat to low and simmer, covered, until soft.

Add the green pepper, celery, aubergines, tomatoes, tomato purée, basil, parsley, seasoning, sugar and stock. Cover the pan and simmer for about 45 minutes, stirring occasionally and adding a little more liquid as required for the sauce. (Bear in mind that the sauce should be thick enough to coat the pasta.)

Adjust seasoning and, if liked, add a few sliced black olives just before serving. *Serves 4.*

# PARSLEY PESTO

*This is certainly not a proper pesto, but I have used the word for want of a better title. Strictly for pesto lovers who miss this delicious pasta sauce when fresh basil is out of season; also for those who are willing to try a version toned down with the somewhat astonishing addition of cottage cheese. Nevertheless, it is still a highly flavoured mixture best served over very hot pasta (as the pesto is not heated). Try it once, and you could become hooked. Serve it with a tossed mixed salad which includes plenty of tomato.*

**60 g (2 oz) parsley sprigs
1 large clove garlic
5 ml (1 tsp) dried basil
125 g (4 oz) coarsely broken walnuts
125 ml (4 fl oz) each olive and
sunflower oil
100 ml (7 tbsp) grated Parmesan cheese
2.5 ml (½ tsp) sea salt and milled black
pepper to taste
500 g (18 oz) cottage cheese
500 g (18 oz) pasta, preferably
wholewheat spaghetti**

Put parsley sprigs, clove of garlic, basil and walnuts into processor fitted with grinding blade and chop. With motor running, add olive and sunflower oils in a slow stream. When thoroughly combined, switch off motor and add Parmesan cheese and seasoning. Process briefly to mix lightly and then scrape the mixture into a bowl. Mix in the cottage cheese, then cover and refrigerate preferably overnight, but return to room temperature and give it a good stir before serving.

Spoon dollops of the sauce on to each serving of freshly cooked, hot pasta on warmed plates. Additional Parmesan cheese is not necessary, but pass the pepper mill at the table.
*Makes about 10 servings.*

# TWO-SAUCE PASTA

*This dish takes a bit of care. The pasta should be home-made and preferably a mixture of green and white fusilli noodles. The tomato sauce requires fresh tomatoes. The spinach and mushroom sauce must be cooked at the last moment. However, if you can claim about 30 minutes of solitude in your kitchen, and have pasta-loving friends with gourmet tastes to feed, try it. Serve with plenty of Parmesan cheese and ground pepper.*

### TOMATO SAUCE
30 ml (2 tbsp) sunflower oil
1 large onion, finely chopped
2 cloves garlic, crushed
500 g (18 oz) ripe and juicy tomatoes, skinned and chopped
25 ml (5 tsp) tomato purée
45 ml (3 tbsp) each white wine and water
5 ml (1 tsp) each sea salt and light brown sugar
2.5 ml (½ tsp) mixed dried herbs
1 bay leaf
100 ml (7 tbsp) chopped parsley

### SPINACH AND MUSHROOM SAUCE
250 g (9 oz) frozen spinach, thawed and very well drained
125 ml (4 fl oz) double cream
125 ml (4 fl oz) buttermilk
2.5 ml (½ tsp) sea salt
25 ml (5 tsp) sweet sherry
a pinch of grated nutmeg
250 g (9 oz) white mushrooms, wiped and coarsely chopped

350 g (12 oz) fusilli noodles

For tomato sauce, heat oil and sauté onion and garlic. Add rest of ingredients, bring to boil, then cover and simmer very gently for about 25 minutes, stirring occasionally to mash tomatoes. When done, sauce should be slightly thickened, but still juicy.

To make the spinach and mushroom sauce, put all ingredients into a medium saucepan first rinsed out with water to prevent mixture from catching on the bottom. Bring to the boil, stirring, then simmer slowly, uncovered. Stir now and then, and cook for about 10 minutes until thickened.

Meanwhile, boil noodles until *al dente* in plenty of salted water with a dash of oil. Drain, then tip into saucepan with tomato sauce. Toss until thoroughly mixed, then pile into large, warmed serving dish. Pour spinach and mushroom sauce over the top or serve separately. Serve at once.
*Serves 6.*

# NOODLE, CHEESE AND VEGETABLE CASSEROLE

*This dish is especially good with a green salad tossed with nuts.*

500 g (18 oz) frozen spinach, thawed
250 g (9 oz) medium ribbon noodles
25 ml (5 tsp) sunflower oil
250 g (9 oz) brown mushrooms, wiped and sliced
1 onion, chopped
5 ml (1 tsp) chopped fresh rosemary needles
25 ml (5 tsp) soy sauce
250 g (9 oz) low-fat soft cheese
4 large spring onions, chopped
2 eggs
250 ml (8 fl oz) buttermilk
sea salt and milled black pepper to taste
2 tomatoes, thinly sliced
2 cloves garlic, crushed
dried oregano for sprinkling
mozzarella cheese for topping
45 ml (3 tbsp) grated Parmesan cheese

Drain spinach in a colander, pressing out all moisture with a wooden spoon. Boil noodles, drain and toss with a dash of oil.

Heat the oil and sauté mushrooms, onion and rosemary. When browned, remove from stove and add soy sauce.

In a large bowl, mix the spinach, soft cheese and spring onions (add some of the green tops). Beat eggs with buttermilk, salt and pepper and add to spinach mixture. Stir in the mushroom mixture and noodles. Spoon into greased, 28 × 23-cm (11 × 9-in) casserole. Cover with tomatoes and sprinkle with garlic and oregano. Finally, top with a thick layer of thinly sliced mozzarella and sprinkle with Parmesan cheese.

Bake at 160°C (325°F, gas 3) for 45 minutes, then turn off oven and leave for about 10 minutes to settle before serving. This dish does not reheat successfully.
*Serves 6.*

---

### ROSEMARY
— • —

Make a habit of adding a sprig or two of fresh rosemary when frying mushrooms. The herb imparts a lovely flavour. Remove the sprigs once the mushrooms have browned.

---

# ITALIAN TOMATO SAUCE WITH FRESH HERBS

*Based on the classic pizzaiola sauce, this is a colourful and aromatic sauce which every cook should have at her/his fingertips. Ignore those recipes which suggest that you add six leaves of basil and a few sprigs of marjoram or a pinch of dried herbs; the tomatoes will simply obliterate their flavour. Herbs should be added with bold generosity, tomatoes should be fresh, not canned, and the sauce simmered very gently to develop the flavours while it thickens. A departure from tradition is the addition of butter beans (I do this for hungry vegetarians) which marry perfectly with the other ingredients. Serve this basic but tasty sauce with home-made pasta, a green salad and grated Parmesan, Romano or Pecorino cheese for a simple, inexpensive meal.*

45 ml (3 tbsp) olive oil
2 large onions, chopped
2-4 cloves garlic, crushed
1 green pepper, seeded and diced
500 g (18 oz) ripe, juicy tomatoes, skinned and chopped
25 ml (5 tsp) tomato purée
2 bay leaves
15 g (½ oz) chopped fresh basil leaves
15 ml (1 tbsp) fresh, chopped oregano leaves
15 ml (1 tbsp) fresh thyme leaves — simply strip them off the stalks
5 ml (1 tsp) light brown sugar
2.5 ml (½ tsp) sea salt and milled black pepper to taste
1.25 ml (¼ tsp) paprika
100 ml (7 tbsp) chopped parsley
45 ml (3 tbsp) white wine
400 g (14 oz) canned choice grade butter beans, drained
a few black olives, slivered

Heat oil and lightly sauté onions, garlic and green pepper. Add remaining ingredients, except beans and olives, bring to the boil, then cover and simmer on low heat for about 30 minutes. Stir occasionally to mash tomatoes. (This sauce is usually cooked uncovered, but this makes it rather too thick if using beans.) Stir in beans and olives, and a dash of water if necessary, and heat through. Serve as suggested.
*Serves 4.*

*Overleaf: Pasta Primavera (p. 33), Creamy Mushroom, Walnut and Pepper Pasta (p. 36) and Italian Tomato Sauce with Fresh Herbs (above).*

# PASTA, VEGETABLE AND LENTIL BAKE

*In this hearty dish, ribbon noodles are layered with vegetables and lentils and topped with a cheese sauce. There are three steps in the preparation, so it does take a little time. However, it may be assembled in advance and baked later, and makes a most economical meal if served with a hot garlic loaf and green salad.*

200 g (7 oz) brown lentils, picked
over and rinsed
30 ml (2 tbsp) sunflower oil
2 onions, chopped
2 cloves garlic, crushed
1 green pepper, seeded and diced
400 g (14 oz) canned tomatoes, chopped
250 g (9 oz) baby marrows, pared
and sliced
90 g (3 oz) shredded spinach leaves or
6 large leaves Swiss chard
5 ml (1 tsp) sea salt and milled black
pepper to taste
10 ml (2 tsp) light brown sugar
5 ml (1 tsp) dried oregano
2.5 ml (½ tsp) dried basil
45 ml (3 tbsp) each white wine and
water
250 g (9 oz) medium ribbon noodles
grated Parmesan cheese

SAUCE
45 ml (3 tbsp) sunflower oil or butter or
equal quantities of each
60 ml (4 tbsp) brown flour
5 ml (1 tsp) mustard powder
500 ml (17 fl oz) milk, preferably heated
2.5 ml (½ tsp) sea salt
125 g (4 oz) finely grated
Cheddar cheese

Cook lentils in 500 ml (17 fl oz) salted water until soft and liquid is absorbed. Meanwhile, heat oil and sauté onions, garlic and green pepper. Add tomatoes plus the juice, baby marrows, spinach, seasoning, sugar, herbs, wine and water. Bring to the boil, then cover and simmer on lowest heat, stirring occasionally, for 25-30 minutes. Stir in cooked lentils. There should be quite a bit of excess liquid to the mixture; this is necessary as the finished dish is baked uncovered, and the juices will then be absorbed.

For sauce, heat oil/butter, stir in flour and mustard, and, when bubbling, add milk slowly, stirring until thickened. Use a balloon whisk. As brown flour takes longer to cook than white flour, allow sauce to simmer gently for a few minutes. Remove from heat and stir in salt and cheese.

Boil noodles in plenty of salted water and drain well.

To assemble, oil a 30 × 20-cm (12 × 8-in) baking dish and cover the base with half the vegetable/lentil mixture. Spread half the noodles over the mixture. Repeat layers. Pour cheese sauce evenly over the top and dust with Parmesan. (Set aside at this stage if preparing in advance.)

Bake the dish, uncovered, at 180°C (350°F, gas 4) for 30 minutes, then turn off oven and leave for a further 15 minutes.
*Makes 6 large servings.*

---

### SPINACH, ONION AND ROSEMARY CREAM SAUCE
·

This is a versatile, rather surprising sauce, distantly related to an aromatic, very thick soup. It is quick and easy to prepare, and makes a nice change from soured cream on baked potatoes. Top the potatoes with a knob of butter first, and serve cottage cheese on the side. It also makes an unusual topping for pasta, finished off with a sprinkling of Parmesan cheese.

25 ml (5 tsp) sunflower oil
30 g (1 oz) butter
2 medium onions, chopped
2 leeks, sliced
2 cloves garlic, crushed
2 fairly large sprigs rosemary
500 g (18 oz) frozen spinach,
thawed
5 ml (1 tsp) sea salt
100 ml (7 tbsp) chopped
parsley
125 ml (4 fl oz) thick soured
cream or double cream

Heat the sunflower oil and butter in a heavy-based saucepan. Add the onions, leeks, garlic and rosemary and sweat over low heat for about 10 minutes until softened. Add the thawed spinach, sea salt and chopped parsley, and cook, stirring, for about 5 minutes. Put aside to cool slightly before tipping the sauce into a blender. Blend until smooth, then return to the saucepan. Add enough of the cream to make a medium-thick sauce, and heat through gently, stirring. Serve at once.
*Makes about 4 large servings.*

---

# VEGETABLE SAUCE

*A chunky, robust sauce, with lots of vegetables and a touch of red wine and herbs. Serve on chosen pasta — spinach noodles are ideal — and top with plenty of feta cheese. This sauce should be made in advance, cooled and then reheated before serving.*

25 ml (5 tsp) each sunflower
and olive oil
3 leeks, sliced
1 onion, chopped
2 cloves garlic, crushed
2 large sticks celery, sliced
2.5 ml (½ tsp) each dried basil, thyme
and oregano
500 g (18 oz) aubergines, cubed
and dégorged
500 g (18 oz) baby marrows, pared
and sliced
125 ml (4 fl oz) tomato passata
125 ml (4 fl oz) red wine
500 ml (17 fl oz) vegetable stock or water
100 ml (7 tbsp) chopped parsley
5 ml (1 tsp) sea salt and milled black
pepper to taste
5 ml (1 tsp) light brown sugar
2 bay leaves
a few leaves of spinach, shredded
250 g (9 oz) whole button mushrooms

500 g (18 oz) spinach noodles, cooked
and drained
feta cheese, rinsed and crumbled

Heat sunflower and olive oils in a very large pan. Add leeks, onion, garlic, celery and herbs. Stir to mix, then cover and sweat over low heat for a few minutes, being careful not to scorch the vegetables and herbs. Add aubergines and marrows, toss until hot, and then add remaining ingredients, except the mushrooms, noodles and feta. Stir to mix, then cover and simmer on lowest heat for about 30 minutes, stirring occasionally — the vegetables will slowly soften and release their juices. Add the mushrooms and simmer the sauce for a further 10 minutes. Transfer to a suitable container and cool.

When reheating, you will probably have to bind the mixture and add a little more liquid — use about 15 ml (1 tbsp) brown flour (you can even use toasted wheatgerm for extra oomph) and enough stock or water to make a good sauce. Bring to the boil, stirring, until sauce thickens. Remove bay leaves and check seasoning before serving. Ladle the sauce over the spinach noodles, and top with crumbled feta cheese.
*Serves 6–8.*

## PASTA WITH MUSHROOM SAUCE

*I find this one a real life-saver. All you need are a few basic ingredients and 20 minutes in hand and you can produce a delicious meal for four to six people. Protein is added by tossing the spaghetti with some chopped nuts and topping each serving with Parmesan, Cheddar or, for a super change, feta cheese.*

300 g (11 oz) spaghetti, fettucini,
tagliatelle or noodles
30 g (1 oz) butter
25 ml (5 tsp) sunflower or olive oil
4 leeks, thinly sliced
2 sticks celery, chopped
1 green pepper, seeded and diced
500 g (18 oz) brown mushrooms,
wiped and sliced
1 sprig fresh rosemary, chopped
2 cloves garlic, crushed
45 ml (3 tbsp) brown flour
375 ml (13 fl oz) hot vegetable or
Marmite stock
45 ml (3 tbsp) soy sauce
45 ml (3 tbsp) sweet sherry
45 ml (3 tbsp) soured cream

Cook pasta or noodles in plenty of salted boiling water. Meanwhile, heat butter and oil in a large saucepan and add leeks, celery and green pepper. When beginning to soften, add mushrooms, rosemary and garlic. Toss over medium heat until smelling really good, then sprinkle in the flour and stir to mix. Slowly add stock, soy sauce and sherry. Stir well and then allow to thicken slowly, half covered.

Just before serving, swirl in the soured cream, then spoon the sauce on to hot, drained pasta or noodles.
*Serves 4–6.*

## PASTA PRIMAVERA

*Primavera, in Italian, means spring and this is the name given to dishes combining spring vegetables and pasta. Both the pasta and choice of vegetables can be varied, so long as the latter are fresh and young. This version is a personal favourite. I make it in summer, rather than in spring, because I like to include lots of fresh basil — it adds a really special fragrance. This dish is fashionably light, quite delicious and please don't be put off by the number of vegetables to clean and steam because you can do without a salad with this meal. Just add a chunk of garlic bread, plenty of grated Parmesan or Pecorino cheese and ground pepper.*

250 g (9 oz) sliced, young green beans
4-6 young carrots, julienned
250 g (9 oz) baby marrows,
pared and julienned
30 ml (2 tbsp) olive oil
1 bunch spring onions
(about 6), chopped
2-3 cloves garlic, crushed
250 g (9 oz) brown or white mushrooms,
wiped and sliced
250 g (9 oz) ripe tomatoes,
skinned and chopped
10 ml (2 tsp) sea salt and a pinch
of sugar
2.5 ml (½ tsp) dried oregano
45 ml (3 tbsp) semi-sweet white wine
350 g (12 oz) vermicelli
30 g (1 oz) butter
15 g (½ oz) chopped fresh basil leaves

Steam the beans, carrots and marrows until just tender, starting with the beans and adding the carrots and marrows after a few minutes. Do not season. They may also be poached in a wide saucepan with just a dash of water.

In another pan, heat the olive oil and sauté the onions, garlic and mushrooms. Add the tomatoes, the steamed vegetables, salt, sugar, oregano and wine. Cover and simmer very gently for about 10 minutes.

Meanwhile, boil the vermicelli until it is *al dente*. Remember that it is thin and cooks very quickly. Drain and tip into a large baking dish. Add butter and basil and toss, using two forks, until well mixed and smelling fabulous — just like pesto. Cover and keep warm in a low oven. When vegetable mixture is ready, pour it over the vermicelli, add an extra knob of butter, toss again with two forks, and serve at once.
*Serves 6.*

## QUICK TOMATO MACARONI CHEESE

*Especially for busy people, this is an old favourite with a different flavour. It makes a simple, satisfying supper and the quantities can be doubled or trebled without adding to the preparation time.*

200 g (7 oz) elbow macaroni
125 g (4 oz) finely grated Cheddar cheese
400 g (14 oz) canned tomatoes
with onions
45 ml (3 tbsp) finely chopped parsley
250 ml (8 fl oz) milk
1 egg
5 ml (1 tsp) mustard powder
5 ml (1 tsp) sea salt and a pinch of
cayenne pepper

TOPPING
100 ml (7 tbsp) fine, fresh wholewheat
breadcrumbs
60 ml (4 tbsp) finely grated
Cheddar cheese
a few slivers of butter

Cook macaroni in boiling salted water. Drain well and tip into a bowl. Mix in the Cheddar, tomatoes and chopped parsley.

Whisk together milk, egg, mustard and seasoning. Stir into macaroni mixture and turn into oiled baking dish — a deep, 20-cm (8-in) pie dish is just right. Mix crumbs and cheese and sprinkle over, then dot with butter. Bake at 160°C (325°F, gas 3) for about 30 minutes or until just set.
*Makes 4 large servings.*

# SPINACH AND MUSHROOM SAUCE

*Fresh spinach is better here, and cheaper, but frozen is fine and quicker. Whichever you use, be sure to drain it very well after cooking. Serve this flavoursome sauce over fettucini, ribbon noodles or spaghetti and top with grated Parmesan, strong Cheddar or crumbled feta cheese.*

**2-3 bunches of young, bright green
spinach or 500 g (18 oz) frozen
spinach, thawed
25 ml (5 tsp) sunflower oil
5 ml (1 tsp) butter
1 large onion, chopped
2 cloves garlic, crushed
1 red pepper, seeded and diced
250 g (9 oz) brown mushrooms,
wiped and sliced
5 ml (1 tsp) finely chopped fresh
rosemary needles
sea salt and milled black pepper to taste
200 ml (7 fl oz) vegetable stock
125 ml (4 fl oz) soured cream
5 ml (1 tsp) Worcestershire sauce
10 ml (2 tsp) cornflour or 25 ml (5 tsp)
toasted wheatgerm**

If using fresh spinach, wash and trim off stalks and thick ribs. You should have 500-600 g (18-21 oz). Put, wet, into a very big saucepan and cook until soft. Drain and press out all moisture, using a colander. Chop finely. If using frozen, thaw quickly by placing the unopened bags in a bowl of cold water. Weight with a saucepan. Drain well.

Heat the sunflower oil and butter in a large frying pan, add onion, garlic and red pepper and allow to soften. Add mushrooms and rosemary and stir until aromatic and lightly browned. Add spinach, seasoning and stock, and simmer until just cooked, stirring occasionally. To bind mixture, mix soured cream, Worcestershire sauce and cornflour or wheatgerm, and add to spinach mixture. Stir until hot and thickened. Serve at once, spooned over pasta.
*Serves 4.*

---

### CHEDDAR CHEESE
#### •

Very well chilled Cheddar grates finely and easily in a processor fitted with the grinding blade. Do a batch and store it in the freezer for instant use.

---

# QUICK VEGETABLE AND BEAN LASAGNE

*No lasagne is really quick. This recipe does, however, offer a few shortcuts. You'll never find this dish in Italy and the ingredients will seem quite improbable, but the result is a very satisfying meal, especially designed for time-strapped cooks. The beans add protein and the dish can be assembled in advance.*

**45 ml (3 tbsp) olive oil
750 g (1½ lb) frozen stir-fry
vegetables, just thawed\*
5 ml (1 tsp) sea salt
2 × 425 g (15 oz) cans choice grade
baked beans in tomato sauce
1 onion, finely chopped
2.5 ml (½ tsp) dried oregano
225-250 g (8-9 oz) lasagne
175 g (6 oz) finely grated strong
Cheddar cheese
grated Parmesan cheese and
toasted sesame seeds for
topping**

SAUCE
**45 ml (3 tbsp) sunflower oil
15 g (½ oz) butter
60 ml (4 tbsp) brown flour
500 ml (17 fl oz) milk
10 ml (2 tsp) prepared mustard
2.5 ml (½ tsp) sea salt**

Heat olive oil. Stir-fry vegetables until just cooked. Remove from heat and add salt, beans, onion and oregano. Set aside.

For sauce, heat oil and butter in heavy-based saucepan. Sprinkle in flour and cook, stirring, until mixture forms a paste. Slowly add heated milk while stirring, or whisking. When smooth, simmer gently for a few minutes to thicken, then add mustard and salt. Whisk before using.

Cook lasagne in boiling, salted water, adding sheets one by one. When just tender, drain and rinse under cold water.

Lightly oil a baking dish. Arrange one third of lasagne on base. Cover with half the vegetable mixture and sprinkle with half the Cheddar cheese. Top with another third of lasagne, then the remaining vegetables and cheese. Top with final layer of lasagne and pour the sauce over. Sprinkle with Parmesan and sesame seeds and bake at 160°C (325°F, gas 3) for 45 minutes.
*Serves 8.*

\* Use a mix including beans, baby marrows, mushrooms, red pepper and celery.

---

# MACARONI, CHEESE AND SPINACH BAKE

*A lovely casserole, with cooked spinach and raw baby marrows layered between pasta, cheese and white sauce. Serve with a crusty loaf, or Greek Garlic Bread (p. 94), and a tomato and basil salad for a perfect mix of flavours and textures.*

**25 ml (5 tsp) olive oil
1 large onion, chopped
2 cloves garlic, crushed
500 g (18 oz) frozen spinach, thawed
sea salt and freshly grated
nutmeg to taste
250 g (9 oz) baby marrows, pared
and coarsely grated
250 g (9 oz) elbow macaroni
175 g (6 oz) finely grated low-fat cheese
(such as mozzarella)
plenty of grated Parmesan or Romano
cheese for topping**

SAUCE
**45 ml (3 tbsp) sunflower oil
15 g (½ oz) butter
60 ml (4 tbsp) brown flour
2.5 ml (½ tsp) dried oregano
500 ml (17 fl oz) milk
2.5 ml (½ tsp) sea salt**

Heat olive oil, and sauté onion and garlic until soft but not browned. Add spinach and stir until just cooked. Remove pan from heat and add salt, nutmeg and marrows (the latter will absorb any excess liquid).

Make sauce by heating oil and butter (you can, of course, use more butter and less oil if you like). Sprinkle in flour and oregano, and when bubbling, add milk slowly. Bring to the boil, stirring, and then allow to simmer for a few minutes. It should be a fairly thin consistency. Season.

Cook macaroni in boiling salted water, and drain thoroughly.

Oil a medium-sized rectangular baking dish or a deep 23-cm (9-in) pie dish. Cover base with half spinach mixture, then add half the cheese, half the macaroni and half the sauce. Repeat layers. (If you'd like a richer, custardy topping, beat an egg into the sauce for the top layer.) Sprinkle generously with Parmesan and bake at 160°C (325°F, gas 3) for 45 minutes. Turn off oven and leave for 15 minutes.
*Makes 6 large servings.*

*Pasta and Aubergine Casserole (p. 36) and Italian Quiche (p. 41).*

# PASTA AND AUBERGINE CASSEROLE

*The flavour of Greece predominates in this substantial, economical dish. Serve with a tossed lettuce and spinach salad and Greek Garlic Bread (p. 94).*

45 ml (3 tbsp) oil, preferably half olive
2 onions, chopped
3 cloves garlic, crushed
575 g (1¼ lb) aubergines, cubed
and dégorged
7.5-10 ml (1½-2 tsp) dried oregano
500 g (18 oz) juicy tomatoes, skinned
and chopped
125 ml (4 fl oz) white wine
2 bay leaves
5 ml (1 tsp) sea salt and milled black
pepper to taste
10 ml (2 tsp) light brown sugar
250 g (9 oz) elbow macaroni

SAUCE
45 ml (3 tbsp) sunflower oil and
a nut of butter
75 ml (5 tbsp) brown flour
750 ml (1¼ pints) milk
sea salt and milled black pepper to taste
1.25 ml (¼ tsp) each ground cinnamon
and grated nutmeg
2 eggs, beaten
45 ml (3 tbsp) grated Parmesan cheese

Heat oil in a very large pan and lightly fry onions and garlic. Add aubergines and oregano and toss for 1-2 minutes, until hot and shiny. Add tomatoes, wine, bay leaves, seasoning and sugar. Cover and simmer on low heat for about 20 minutes, stirring occasionally to mash tomatoes. Add a dash of water if mixture seems dry. It should be thick and juicy, but not watery.

Meanwhile, cook pasta in salted water with a dash of oil. Drain well.

Make sauce by melting oil and butter, stirring in flour and slowly adding milk. Stir until smooth and then simmer for a few minutes until medium-thick. Add seasoning and spices. Spoon a little sauce on to beaten eggs, then add to sauce with half the cheese and whisk to mix.

Remove bay leaves from aubergines. Lightly oil a deep, 30 × 20-cm (12 × 8-in) baking dish. Cover base with half aubergine mixture, top with half pasta, then repeat layers. Pour white sauce over, and then sprinkle with remaining Parmesan. Bake, uncovered, at 160°C (325°F, gas 3) for 50 minutes, then turn off oven and leave for 15 minutes.
*Makes 8 large servings.*

---

## WHITE SAUCE

In keeping with the unrefined ingredients used in this book, I have broken with tradition and, instead of using butter and white flour for making white/béchamel sauces, I have substituted oil, or a mixture of butter and oil, and plain brown flour. This results in a sauce that is not white, but slightly speckled and somewhat thinner, and which needs extra simmering to cook the flour and obtain the right consistency. The flavour, although not delicate, is fine (especially if used in a cheesy casserole) and in view of the fact that meals without meat or fish often rely heavily on dairy products for protein, it makes sense to cut down on saturated fats when possible. Cordon bleu cooks may be dismayed by this method, but in the cuisine of certain countries, butter is never used in white sauces.

---

# PASTA, MUSHROOM AND RICOTTA BAKE

*Devised with an eye to short-term preparation, this casserole conveniently dispenses with the making of the sauces which usually accompany baked pasta dishes. When you're not in a hurry, however, use a fragrant, slow-simmered, home-made tomato sauce. Serve with a tossed green salad — either add croûtons to the salad, or serve Italian breadsticks on the side.*

25 ml (5 tsp) sunflower oil
5 ml (1 tsp) butter
1 large onion, finely chopped
250 g (9 oz) brown mushrooms, wiped
and finely chopped
2 sprigs fresh rosemary
400 g (14 oz) ricotta cheese
45 ml (3 tbsp) chopped parsley
25 ml (5 tsp) soy sauce
250 ml (8 fl oz) soured cream
5 ml (1 tsp) sea salt
250 g (9 oz) medium ribbon noodles
400 g (14 oz) canned tomatoes
with onions
5 ml (1 tsp) dried basil
grated Parmesan cheese or
any low-fat cheese

Heat oil and butter and add onion, mushrooms and rosemary. Keep heat low to allow mushrooms to soften without burning, as they will initially absorb a lot of oil. When tender and cooked, there should be no juices left in the pan. Tip into a large mixing bowl and mix in the ricotta, parsley, soy sauce, cream and salt.

Boil noodles in plenty of salted water with a dash of oil. Drain well and stir into mushroom mixture. Turn into oiled 30 × 20-cm (12 × 8-in) baking dish, spreading evenly.

Mix tomatoes and basil, and spread over the top. Because ricotta is a fairly firm cheese, the topping will not sink in. Sprinkle plenty of Parmesan (or chosen low-fat cheese) over the top and bake at 160°C (325°F, gas 3) for 45 minutes.
*Serves 6.*

---

# CREAMY MUSHROOM, WALNUT AND PEPPER PASTA

*Unlike many pasta dishes made with vegetables and sauces, which have to be baked, this dish is quickly prepared on the hob. The cream and walnuts make it rich, but it's a lovely indulgence when you want a quick meal.*

250 g (9 oz) pasta (spinach or
egg noodles, fettucini or
wholewheat spaghetti)
30 ml (2 tbsp) olive oil
1 small onion, chopped
2 leeks, sliced
2 cloves garlic, crushed
1 large red pepper, seeded and diced
1 large green pepper, seeded and diced
2.5 ml (½ tsp) each dried basil
and oregano
250 g (9 oz) brown mushrooms,
wiped and sliced
30 ml (2 tbsp) sweet sherry
250 ml (8 fl oz) soured cream
25 ml (5 tsp) grated Parmesan cheese
5 ml (1 tsp) sea salt and milled black
pepper to taste
60 g (2 oz) chopped walnuts (optional)

Cook pasta in plenty of salted water with a dash of oil. Meanwhile, heat oil, add onion, leeks, garlic, peppers and herbs, turn heat to lowest, cover and allow to sweat until softened, shaking pan occasionally. Add mushrooms and sherry and toss, still over low heat, until mushrooms are just beginning to shrink. Stir in well-drained noodles, cream, cheese, seasoning and walnuts, if using. Heat through gently until pasta is coated with sauce. Do not overcook.
*Serves 4–6.*

# TWO-SAUCE NOODLE CASSEROLE

*This is an ideal dish for informal entertaining as it can be assembled in advance. Hot Pitta Bread (p. 93) with herb butter and a green salad tossed with sunflower seeds make particularly good accompaniments. As it is a dairy-rich dish, use low-fat milk for sauce.*

**250 g (9 oz) medium spinach noodles**
**a little grated Parmesan cheese**

MUSHROOM SAUCE
45 ml (3 tbsp) sunflower oil
(or half olive)
1 large onion, chopped
2 cloves garlic, crushed
1 green pepper, seeded and diced
250 g (9 oz) brown mushrooms,
wiped and sliced
250 g (9 oz) ripe tomatoes, skinned
and chopped
25 ml (5 tsp) tomato purée
10 ml (2 tsp) vegetable salt or
5 ml (1 tsp) sea salt, and freshly
milled black pepper to taste
5 ml (1 tsp) brown sugar
2 bay leaves
2.5 ml (½ tsp) dried oregano
45 ml (3 tbsp) medium dry white wine

CHEESE SAUCE
25 ml (5 tsp) sunflower oil and
a nut of butter
60 ml (4 tbsp) brown flour
5 ml (1 tsp) mustard powder
500 ml (17 fl oz) skimmed milk
125 g (4 oz) grated Cheddar cheese
sea salt and milled black pepper to taste

Boil noodles, drain and toss with a dash of oil. Leave in colander and set aside.

For mushroom sauce, heat oil and soften onion, garlic and green pepper. Add mushrooms and, when softening, add rest of the ingredients. Cover and simmer for 20 minutes, stirring occasionally. Remove bay leaves. For cheese sauce, heat oil and butter, stir in flour and mustard, and when nut-brown, add milk slowly. Cook until thickened, then add cheese and seasoning.

Oil a 28 × 18-cm (11 × 7-in) baking dish or a deep, 23-cm (9-in) pie dish. Cover base with half the mushroom sauce and top with half the noodles. Repeat layers. Pour cheese sauce over top, sprinkle with Parmesan and bake, uncovered, at 180°C (350°F, gas 4) for 30 minutes. Turn off oven, and leave for 15 minutes.
*Serves 6.*

# PASTA WITH VEGETABLES AND HERBS

*This is a favourite, one-saucepan pasta dish in which fusilli or spiral noodles, mushrooms and baby marrows are folded into a robustly flavoured butter and oil sauce. It is very easy and exceptionally quick to make: the herby sauce is mixed in advance in order to develop the flavour and the final cook-up takes but a few minutes, if using home-made pasta. Hand the cheese separately and a loaf of crusty white bread, and, if you like, a Greek salad with plenty of feta cheese, in which case, omit the Parmesan.*

SAUCE
30 ml (2 tbsp) olive oil
30 g (1 oz) butter
100 ml (7 tbsp) finely chopped
parsley
2 cloves garlic, crushed
5 ml (1 tsp) dried oregano*
2.5 ml (½ tsp) dried basil*
1.25 ml (¼ tsp) dried thyme*

250 g (9 oz) fusilli or spiral noodles
45 ml (3 tbsp) olive oil
45 ml (3 tbsp) dry vermouth
250 g (9 oz) brown mushrooms,
wiped and sliced
250 g (9 oz) baby marrows,
pared and julienned
5 ml (1 tsp) sea salt
plenty of freshly grated Parmesan or
Romano or Pecorino cheese

For the sauce, heat the olive oil and butter in a small saucepan over low heat. Add parsley, garlic and the herbs and stir for 1 minute, then remove from stove, cover and leave to steep for at least 1 hour.

Just before dinner, cook pasta, and at the same time cook the vegetables. Heat the olive oil with the vermouth in a very large saucepan (use one that is pretty enough to take to the table). Add vegetables and salt and toss over medium heat until just softened.

Using a two-pronged fork, fork the well-drained pasta into the vegetable mixture, and then add the herb sauce. Toss together gently until just heated through and smelling gorgeous, and then serve at once. Hand the chosen cheese separately for sprinkling.
*Serves 4.*

* Be sure to use absolutely level measures of these herbs or the flavour will be too pronounced. Less is better than more.

# EASY PIZZA WITH WHOLEWHEAT CRUST

*There are surely more varieties of pizza than there are roads in Rome — not only with regard to what you put on top, but also what you do to the base. Traditionally, it's a yeast dough which I, personally, find too heavy and often very dry. The following is a quick alternative.*

CRUST
125 g (4 oz) wholewheat flour
125 g (4 oz) white flour
2.5 ml (½ tsp) sea salt
5 ml (1 tsp) baking powder
75 ml (5 tbsp) sunflower oil
100 ml (7 tbsp) skimmed milk
10 ml (2 tsp) lemon juice

TOPPING
100 ml (7 tbsp) tomato sauce
10 ml (2 tsp) Worcestershire sauce
2.5 ml (½ tsp) each dried oregano
and thyme
2 tomatoes, sliced
1 onion, coarsely grated
2 cloves garlic, crushed
grated Cheddar and Parmesan cheese*
black olives and cooked
mushrooms (optional)
a little olive oil
2.5 ml (½ tsp) garlic salt

To make the crust, mix flours, salt and baking powder. Add oil, milk and lemon juice. Quickly mix to a ball (use an electric beater if possible) and press evenly on to the base of a lightly oiled 33 × 20-cm (13 × 8-in) Swiss roll tin, or a pizza pan.

Mix tomato sauce, Worcestershire sauce and herbs and spread over dough, right to the edges. Cover with tomatoes, onion and garlic. Sprinkle thickly with Cheddar cheese and dust with Parmesan. Top pizza with olives and mushrooms, if desired. Drizzle with olive oil, sprinkle with garlic salt and bake at 200°C (400°F, gas 6) for about 30 minutes, until bubbly and cooked. Cut into fingers and serve very hot.
*Serves 6–8.*

* Or use mozzarella cheese for a perfect topping. It melts to form a golden-brown blanket. Use sliced rather than grated.

*Overleaf: Pasta, Vegetable and Lentil bake (p. 32), Pasta with Herbs and Eggs (p. 27) and Easy Pizza with Wholewheat Crust (above).*

# FAVOURITE MACARONI CHEESE

*Quite possibly, the last time you ate macaroni cheese was at school. And quite possibly this put you off it forever, which is a pity because it can be jolly tasty, especially if, when making it, you follow the one cardinal rule — never overcook the macaroni or it will never marry with the sauce and you'll end up with that dry, stick-like school affair. The pasta must be al dente. The second recipe includes eggs, but is simpler and easier than the first in that you don't have to make a sauce. Take your pick, but in neither case should you rinse the macaroni after draining as that prevents the sauce from coating it.*

### RECIPE 1

25 ml (5 tsp) sunflower oil
30 g (1 oz) butter
60 ml (4 tbsp) white flour
750 ml (1¼ pints) milk (skimmed
or semi-skimmed)
5 ml (1 tsp) sea salt
2 pickling-size onions, coarsely grated
10 ml (2 tsp) prepared mustard
125 g (4 oz) finely grated Cheddar cheese
a large pinch of cayenne pepper

#### TOPPING
60 g (2 oz) fine, stale plain brown
breadcrumbs
60 ml (4 tbsp) finely grated
Cheddar cheese
25 ml (5 tsp) grated Parmesan cheese
250 g (9 oz) elbow macaroni
a few slivers of butter

First, make a white sauce by melting the oil and the butter, stirring in the flour, and then slowly adding the milk. Stir until smooth. Simmer for a few minutes until thickened, then remove from the stove and stir in the salt, onions, mustard, Cheddar cheese and cayenne pepper.

Prepare topping by mixing breadcrumbs and both cheeses.

Cook pasta in boiling salted water and drain thoroughly to avoid adding any water to the dish. Toss drained pasta with cheese sauce, and then spoon into a lightly oiled baking dish — 30 × 20-cm (12 × 8-in) dish or a deep, 23-cm (9-in) pie dish. Sprinkle with the prepared topping and dot with slivers of butter.

Bake at 160°C (325°F, gas 3) for about 30 minutes until just bubbling. Do not overbake.
*Serves 6 with a salad.*

### RECIPE 2

250 g (9 oz) elbow macaroni
1.25 ml (¼ tsp) freshly grated nutmeg
2 eggs
500 ml (17 fl oz) milk (skimmed
or semi-skimmed)
5 ml (1 tsp) sea salt
125 g (4 oz) finely grated Cheddar cheese

#### TOPPING
60 g (2 oz) finely grated Cheddar cheese
paprika
a few slivers of butter

Cook macaroni in boiling salted water until *al dente*, drain very well, and then place in a lightly oiled 23-cm (9-in) pie dish. Sprinkle with grated nutmeg.

Beat eggs with milk and salt and stir in cheese. Pour over macaroni, sprinkle with topping of Cheddar and paprika, and dot with butter. Bake at 160°C (325°F, gas 3) for 30 minutes or until just set. Do not overbake.
*Serves 6 with a salad.*

# PASTA RATATOUILLE WITH MARINATED FETA

*This is a good recipe for the hurried or weight-conscious cook. The latter could use Parmesan cheese instead of the feta. However, this is a marvellous way of treating feta ('cured' in herbs and oil), which can be used in any dish or salad in which a topping of feta is required.*

### RATATOUILLE

1 medium onion, chopped
3-4 leeks, sliced
500 g (18 oz) baby marrows,
pared and sliced
750 g (1½ lb) aubergines, cubed
and dégorged
500 g (18 oz) juicy tomatoes, skinned and
chopped (not canned)
2 green or red peppers, or one of each,
seeded and diced
3-4 cloves garlic, crushed
4 bay leaves
5 ml (1 tsp) each dried oregano
and thyme
10 ml (2 tsp) each sea salt and
light brown sugar
milled black pepper to taste
100 ml (7 tbsp) olive oil
400-500 g (14-18 oz) pasta of choice

Put all the ingredients, except the pasta, into a really big saucepan as the mixture is very bulky to start with, reducing only when it has cooked for a while. Toss all the ingredients until mixed, bring to the boil, and then cover and simmer over very low heat until the vegetables are tender — for 40-50 minutes. Stir occasionally, but be careful not to break up the vegetables. You should not need to add any liquid as the vegetables should draw their own juices. Add a few black olives, if liked.

Cook pasta just before serving, and ladle sauce over each portion. Top with the marinated feta cheese.
*Serves 6–8.*

### MARINATED FETA

*To make this slightly more economical, the feta will not be completely covered with oil; so the jar should be turned upside down now and then to allow all the cheese to be submerged. It should be made about two days in advance and kept in the refrigerator.*

400 g (14 oz) feta cheese, rinsed
4 whole cloves garlic
a few black olives
2 sprigs fresh rosemary
4 bay leaves
about 200 ml (7 fl oz) each olive and
sunflower oil
5 ml (1 tsp) dried oregano
1.25 ml (¼ tsp) dried thyme
45 ml (3 tbsp) lemon juice

Pack the feta cheese into a wide-mouthed, 750-ml (1¼-pint) glass jar together with the garlic cloves, olives, sprigs of rosemary and bay leaves. Mix the olive and sunflower oils, dried herbs and lemon juice and pour over the cheese. Seal the jar and refrigerate.

---

### SALT
·

Use pure sea salt (not table salt), either fine or coarse. Grind coarse salt in a salt mill at the table — you will use far less. Apart from sodium chloride, sea salt also contains certain minerals and trace elements, so it's much healthier than table salt. It is available, reasonably priced, from health-food shops and in better supermarkets.

# ASPARAGUS AND SPRING ONION QUICHE

*Serve as a light meal with a salad of lettuce, grated baby marrows and bean sprouts.*

### CRUST
175 g (6 oz) white or brown flour
2.5 ml (½ tsp) sea salt
2.5 ml (½ tsp) baking powder
100 ml (7 tbsp) sunflower oil
a squeeze of lemon juice
10 ml (2 tsp) cornflour

### FILLING
450 g (1 lb) canned asparagus spears, well drained
6 spring onions, chopped
250 g (9 oz) low-fat soft cheese
2.5 ml (½ tsp) dried tarragon
2.5 ml (½ tsp) sea salt and milled black pepper to taste
3 eggs
125 ml (4 fl oz) milk
125 ml (4 fl oz) single cream
25 ml (5 tsp) chopped parsley
paprika and grated Gruyère cheese

To make crust, sift flour, salt and baking powder. Add oil, 45 ml (3 tbsp) iced water and lemon juice. Mix lightly with a fork, shape into a ball and roll out thinly between two sheets of greaseproof paper. Line a deep, 23-cm (9-in) flan tin, prick well and bake at 200°C (400°F, gas 6) for 15 minutes. Remove and dust base with cornflour. Cool. If asparagus stalks are thick, cut in half lengthways. Arrange on crust, with spring onions.

Beat soft cheese with tarragon, salt and pepper. Beat in eggs, one at a time, followed by the milk, cream and parsley. Pour carefully on to crust, dust with paprika and sprinkle with Gruyère. Reduce oven temperature to 180°C (350°F, gas 4) and heat a baking tray for a few minutes. Place flan tin on the hot tray and bake for 45 minutes or until set.
*Serves 6–8.*

---

### SAUTÉ AND SWEAT
•

In the former, the vegetables are lightly browned, whereas in the latter they are cooked gently, covered with a lid, to allow them to soften in their own juices.

---

# SPINACH AND BROWN MUSHROOM QUICHE

*A substantial, large, cheesy and herby quiche which reheats well.*

### PASTRY
100 g (3½ oz) each white and wholewheat flour
pinch of sea salt
125 g (4 oz) butter
a squeeze of lemon juice
1 egg white (reserve the yolk)

### FILLING
2 × 250 g (9 oz) packets frozen spinach, thawed
1.25 ml (¼ tsp) sea salt
2.5 ml (½ tsp) dried dill
25 ml (5 tsp) sunflower oil
30 g (1 oz) butter
250 g (9 oz) brown mushrooms, wiped and roughly chopped
2 leeks, sliced
1 small onion, chopped
1 sprig fresh rosemary
sea salt and milled black pepper to taste
250 ml (8 fl oz) milk
2 eggs plus reserved yolk
125 ml (4 fl oz) soured cream
5 ml (1 tsp) French mustard
100 g (3½ oz) Gruyère or Cheddar cheese, grated
2.5 ml (½ tsp) dried oregano

To make the pastry, mix flours and salt. Rub in butter until crumbly, then bind with 75 ml (5 tbsp) iced water and lemon juice. Form pastry into a ball, chill for about 30 minutes, then roll out and line a deep 28-cm (11-in) quiche tin. Prick well and bake at 200°C (400°F, gas 6) for 20 minutes. Brush with the lightly beaten egg white, and return to oven for 5 minutes.

For the filling, drain spinach well, pressing out all moisture, then season with the sea salt and dried dill. Heat the oil and butter and sauté mushrooms, leeks, onion and rosemary. When half-soft, remove the rosemary and season the mixture lightly. Beat the milk with eggs and reserved egg yolk, soured cream, mustard and more seasoning, if needed.

Spread drained spinach over crust and spoon mushroom mixture over. Pour egg mixture over, sprinkle with chosen cheese and the oregano, and then bake at 160°C (325°F, gas 3) for 45 minutes or until set.
*Serves 8.*

---

# ITALIAN QUICHE

*Baked in a 30-cm (12-in) pizza pan, this is a hearty quiche with a wholewheat crust and a ratatouille-type filling. Serve with a salad.*

### PROCESSOR PASTRY
125 g (4 oz) wholewheat flour
60 g (2 oz) plain flour
2.5 ml (½ tsp) sea salt
125 g (4 oz) butter, diced
10 ml (2 tsp) lemon juice
15 ml (1 tbsp) extra flour

### FILLING
45 ml (3 tbsp) olive oil
2 leeks, chopped
1 small onion, chopped
1 green pepper, seeded and diced
2 cloves garlic, crushed
250 g (9 oz) baby marrows, pared and diced
250 g (9 oz) aubergines, diced
2.5 ml (½ tsp) sea salt and milled black pepper to taste
45 ml (3 tbsp) chopped parsley
2.5 ml (½ tsp) dried oregano
1.25 ml (¼ tsp) dried basil
125 g (4 oz) cream cheese
375 ml (13 fl oz) milk
3 eggs
1.25 ml (¼ tsp) sea salt
1 large tomato, thinly sliced
125 g (4 oz) grated Cheddar cheese
25 ml (5 tsp) grated Parmesan cheese

To make pastry, use grinding blade of processor to mix flours, salt and butter until finely blended. With motor running, add lemon juice and 30-45 ml (2-3 tbsp) cold water. Stop as soon as it forms a ball, turn out on to floured board and roll out, using floured rolling pin. Using fingers, press into pizza pan, flute edges, prick well and chill.

To make filling, heat oil in a large pan and sauté leeks, onion, green pepper and garlic. When translucent, add marrows and aubergines, then season with salt and pepper. Cover and cook over low heat, stirring occasionally, until soft. Spoon into a bowl and add parsley and dried herbs. Cool.

Bake crust at 200°C (400°F, gas 6) for 12 minutes. Distribute about 15 ml (1 tbsp) flour over base, using pastry brush. Spoon in filling.

For custard, beat cream cheese, milk, eggs and salt. Arrange tomato over vegetables, pour custard over, sprinkle with cheeses and bake at 180°C (350°F, gas 4) for 30-35 minutes. Turn off oven and leave for 20 minutes to settle.
*Serves 8.*

# RICE & OTHER GRAINS

## NUTTY BARLEY AND VEGETABLE BAKE

*Barley is a sadly neglected grain which most people use only in soups. This is a pity for it has a marvellous nutty texture and is very nutritious. Try serving it instead of rice, or in a salad. Barley is also very satisfying, especially when used in a vegetable casserole. Cinnamon-baked pumpkin and creamed spinach are good accompaniments.*

45 ml (3 tbsp) sunflower oil
2 large onions, chopped
2 sticks celery, plus some
leaves, chopped
1 green pepper, seeded and diced
250 g (9 oz) brown mushrooms,
wiped and sliced
250 g (9 oz) baby marrows, pared
and sliced
5 ml (1 tsp) mixed dried herbs
5 ml (1 tsp) sea salt
275 g (10 oz) pearl barley, rinsed
and drained
750 ml (1¼ pints) Marmite stock
60 g (2 oz) toasted sunflower seeds
(or more, if you like them)
2 tomatoes, thinly sliced into rounds
for topping
plenty of sliced or grated mozzarella or
Cheddar or low-fat cheese for topping

Heat oil and sauté onions, celery and green pepper. Add mushrooms, marrows and herbs and toss over low heat until just wilting and smelling good. Add salt and spoon mixture into a rectangular baking dish, about 30 × 20 cm (12 × 8 in). Add barley, stock and sunflower seeds and mix with a fork until well combined, spreading evenly. Cover securely and bake at 160°C (325°F, gas 3) for 1 hour. Uncover and top with tomatoes. Cover with cheese, and bake, uncovered, for 20-30 minutes more. *Serves 8.*

*Nutty Vegetable Rice with Stuffed Mushrooms (p. 48).*

43

# NUTTY RICE AND MUSHROOM CASSEROLE

*In this dish, the vegetables are first sautéed and then baked in stock with the uncooked rice and herbs, resulting in maximum flavour with the minimum of fuss and a lovely aroma while it is in the oven. The omelette topping, cut into strips, finishes it off beautifully.*

60 ml (4 tbsp) sunflower oil
1 onion, chopped
2 leeks, sliced
2 cloves garlic, crushed
250 g (9 oz) brown mushrooms,
wiped and sliced
4 young carrots, julienned
2 sticks celery, plus some
leaves, chopped
300 g (11 oz) brown rice
15 g (½ oz) chopped parsley
800 ml (27 fl oz) hot vegetable or
Marmite stock
5 ml (1 tsp) sea salt and a little milled
black pepper to taste
30 ml (2 tbsp) finely chopped
fresh herbs*
30 ml (2 tbsp) soy sauce
60 g (2 oz) toasted almond strips
a few nuts of butter

OMELETTES
8-10 eggs
sea salt and milled black pepper to taste
a little sesame oil

Heat oil in large pan and lightly fry onion, leeks and garlic. Add mushrooms, carrots and celery and stir-fry for a few minutes until glistening, smelling good and beginning to soften. Spoon into a 30×20-cm (12×8-in) baking dish. Add the rice, parsley, stock, seasoning and herbs. Stir with a wooden spoon until well combined, then cover and bake at 160°C (325°F, gas 3) for about 1 hour 10 minutes, until rice is cooked and stock absorbed. Fork in soy sauce, almonds and butter.

During last few minutes of baking, make two omelettes by mixing eggs lightly with a little water, salt and pepper. Do not overbeat. Cook half the egg mixture in a greased pan at a time. (Do use sesame oil.) When just set, tilt pan and roll omelette over a few times. Remove to plate and slice thinly. Arrange slices on top of casserole.
*Serves 6.*

* I use a mixture of rosemary, thyme, marjoram and oregano.

---

---

# RICE WITH LENTILS, MUSHROOMS AND ALMONDS

*Served with a creamy green salad, this vegetarian main dish is a real delight.*

200 g (7 oz) brown lentils, picked
over and rinsed
1 bay leaf
a few nuts of butter
5 ml (1 tsp) ground cumin
2 pinches of sea salt
300 g (11 oz) brown rice
5 ml (1 tsp) mixed dried herbs
30 g (1 oz) butter
25 ml (5 tsp) sunflower oil
2 onions, thinly sliced
1 red pepper, seeded and sliced
300-400 g (11-14 oz) brown mushrooms,
wiped and sliced
2 sticks celery, chopped
100 ml (7 tbsp) chopped parsley
125 g (4 oz) mung bean sprouts
45 ml (3 tbsp) soy sauce*
45 g (1½ oz) halved, toasted
almonds

Put lentils into saucepan with 500 ml (17 fl oz) water, bay leaf, a nut of butter, cumin and a pinch of salt. Bring to boil, then cover and simmer gently for about 50 minutes until water is absorbed and lentils are soft.

Meanwhile, cook the rice in another saucepan with 850 ml (30 fl oz) water, a nut of butter, a pinch of sea salt and mixed herbs, and simmer, covered, over low heat for about 45 minutes.

---

Toss lentils and rice together and spoon into a large, buttered baking dish, discarding bay leaf. Cover and keep warm in low oven, or set aside to reheat gently later.

To prepare vegetables, heat butter and oil in a large frying pan and add onions and red pepper. When soft and browning, increase heat and add mushrooms, celery and parsley. Stir-fry for 5 minutes, then add sprouts and soy sauce. Reduce heat and cook for a further 2 minutes, tossing with wooden spoon. Pour mixture over warm rice and lentils and scatter with almonds.
*Serves 8–10.*

* Soy sauce should season the dish sufficiently, so taste before adding salt.

# ONE-POT MUSHROOM RISOTTO

*A convenience dish which makes a lovely, light meal. The correct rice for risottos is the Italian Arborio, but I have substituted brown rice.*

30 ml (2 tbsp) sunflower oil
30 g (1 oz) butter
1 large onion, finely chopped
2 cloves garlic, crushed
250 g (9 oz) brown mushrooms,
wiped and sliced
200 g (7 oz) brown rice
1 red pepper, seeded and diced
5 ml (1 tsp) chopped, fresh
rosemary needles
550 ml (18 fl oz) hot Marmite stock
45 ml (3 tbsp) finely chopped parsley
25 ml (5 tsp) soy sauce
25 ml (5 tsp) sweet sherry
125 g (4 oz) bean or other sprouts
toasted almond strips (optional) and an
extra knob of butter (plain or flavoured
with herbs and garlic)
fried eggs for topping

Heat oil and butter in large frying pan with lid and sauté onion and garlic. Add mushrooms, rice, red pepper and rosemary and stir-fry over low heat until glistening and aromatic. Add hot stock, parsley, soy sauce and sherry. Stir through quickly with a fork, then cover and simmer on very low heat for about 50 minutes or until rice is tender. Do not stir, but towards the end of the cooking period, check if you need a little more stock. Fork in bean sprouts. If using almonds, add them now with extra butter; otherwise, spoon mixture into a serving dish, top with eggs and serve at once.
*Serves 6–8.*

# SPICED RICE, LENTILS AND VEGETABLES WITH YOGHURT

*This dish is neither a pilaff nor a biryani, but simply an aromatic mixture of Eastern ingredients in which Basmati rice, laced with spices, is served on a dish of lentils cooked with butternut squash and tomatoes, drizzled with a nutty yoghurt topping and finished off with fresh mint. It is a wonderfully fragrant dish and despite the rather long list of ingredients, it really is quite simple to prepare. Furthermore, I find it does not have to be cooked and eaten immediately — often a daunting factor. Each component is prepared separately and then heated through just before dinner. Not authentic, but fragrant and very tasty.*

### TOPPING
500 ml (17 fl oz) Bulgarian yoghurt
45 g (1½ oz) desiccated coconut
75 g (2½ oz) raisins, plumped in hot water and drained
60 g (2 oz) finely chopped, toasted almonds
10 ml (2 tsp) thin honey
a pinch of sea salt
chopped fresh mint

### RICE
200 g (7 oz) Basmati rice, carefully picked over
25 ml (5 tsp) sunflower oil
30 g (1 oz) butter
1 large onion, finely chopped
2 sticks cinnamon
4 whole cloves
2.5 ml (½ tsp) turmeric
5 ml (1 tsp) ground coriander
5 ml (1 tsp) sea salt

### LENTILS
25 ml (5 tsp) sunflower oil
1 large onion, finely chopped
5 ml (1 tsp) leaf masala (or more if you want it hot)
2.5 ml (½ tsp) turmeric
5 ml (1 tsp) each ground ginger and fennel
250 g (9 oz) coarsely grated, peeled butternut squash
200 g (7 oz) firm tomatoes, coarsely grated, and skin discarded
200 g (7 oz) brown or green lentils, picked over and rinsed
5 ml (1 tsp) each sea salt and sugar

Prepare the topping first by mixing all the ingredients together, except the chopped fresh mint. Cover and chill.

To prepare rice, wash well, then cover with cold water. Pour off any husks or bits that float to the top. Soak for 30 minutes. Drain. Heat oil and butter and braise (or soften) onion. Add spices and sizzle on low heat for 1-2 minutes. Add rice, 750 ml (1¼ pints) water and salt. Bring to the boil, cover and simmer gently for 20 minutes. Turn off heat and stand for 10 minutes, or longer if preparing in advance. Remove spices.

To cook lentils, heat oil in large frying pan with lid, add onion and cook until wilted. Add spices and fry for 1-2 minutes to release flavours. Add remaining ingredients, plus 500 ml (17 fl oz) water, bring to the boil, then cover and simmer on very low heat for 1 hour.

When ready, both the rice and the lentil mixtures should be just moist enough to stand gentle reheating without any danger of scorching. When just heated through, pile rice into a large, warmed baking dish. Spoon the lentil mixture over the rice. If liked, keep warm, covered, in a low oven for a short while.

Just before serving, drizzle over some of yoghurt topping and sprinkle with mint. Serve rest of yoghurt topping separately. *Serves 6.*

# ORIENTAL RICE

*A simple dish, combining rice with steamed vegetables, lentil sprouts, soy sauce and seeds or nuts. With the addition of eggs, it makes a nourishing, light meal.*

225 g (8 oz) brown rice
250 g (9 oz) sliced, young green beans
4-6 young carrots, julienned
2 sticks celery, plus some leaves, chopped
60 ml (4 tbsp) sunflower oil
20 ml (4 tsp) dark sesame oil
1 large bunch spring onions, chopped
250 g (9 oz) brown mushrooms, wiped and sliced
25 ml (5 tsp) sweet sherry
125 g (4 oz) lentil sprouts
45 ml (3 tbsp) soy sauce
60 ml (4 tbsp) toasted sesame seeds or
60 g (2 oz) toasted slivered almonds or toasted sunflower seeds
4 eggs, poached, or made into an omelette, thinly sliced

Place rice in saucepan with 625 ml (21 fl oz) water and 2.5 ml (½ tsp) salt, bring to the boil, then cover and simmer very gently until cooked and water is absorbed.

Meanwhile, poach or steam (covered, in very little water) the beans, carrots and celery (cook the beans for a few minutes before adding the carrots and celery) until crisply tender and set aside. Do not season.

Heat both oils in a large frying pan and sauté onions. Add mushrooms and when softening, add sherry and cook gently for a minute or two to bring out the flavour. Fork in steamed vegetables, lentil sprouts, soy sauce and seeds or nuts. Turn into large, warmed baking dish and fork in the rice. If mixture needs extra moisture, toss in a nut of butter, then cover and keep warm in a low oven. Prepare eggs, arrange on top of rice and serve at once, with extra soy sauce if liked.
*Makes 4 large servings.*

# KITCHEREE WITH FRIED EGGS

*From Egypt to India, the nourishing combination of rice and lentils is eaten in many forms, usually with spices and/or hot sauces. The following version is lightly spiced and makes a very satisfying and economical meal. Serve with a bowl of Bulgarian yoghurt and a layered tomato and onion salad.*

45 ml (3 tbsp) sunflower oil
2 large onions, sliced into thin rings
2.5 ml (½ tsp) masala for medium curry
5 ml (1 tsp) each ground cumin and fennel
2 bay leaves
2 sticks cinnamon
4 whole cloves
150 g (5 oz) brown rice
150 g (5 oz) brown lentils, picked over and rinsed
5 ml (1 tsp) sea salt
2 nuts of butter
4 fried eggs

Heat oil in large frying pan with a lid. Add onions and sauté until golden. Turn heat to low, add spices and sizzle for a minute or two. Add remaining ingredients, except butter and eggs, plus 850 ml (29 fl oz) boiling water, bring to the boil, stirring to mix, then cover securely and simmer on lowest possible heat for about 1 hour, until rice and lentils are cooked and all liquid absorbed. If working ahead, turn off heat and leave for full flavour to develop.

To serve, remove spices and reheat over low heat. Fork in the butter and spoon on to large, warmed serving platter. Top with eggs and serve as suggested.
*Serves 4.*

# BULGUR, LENTIL AND TAHINI PILAFF

*This absolutely delicious dish combines 'health foods' which are sure to be unfamiliar to many. The result is so good and the flavours so subtle, that you're bound to be quizzed about the ingredients. And once you've discovered how easy it is to prepare, you're sure to make it often. I like to top this pilaff with either fried or hard-boiled eggs for extra protein. Serve it with buttered corn or a green salad, or omit the eggs and serve it cold as a salad.*

150 g (5 oz) green lentils, picked
over and rinsed
2.5 ml (1/2 tsp) each sea salt and
turmeric
45 ml (3 tbsp) sunflower oil
1 bunch spring onions, chopped
2 cloves garlic, crushed
1 green or red pepper, seeded
and diced
5-7.5 ml (1-1½ tsp) each ground cumin,
coriander and fennel
150 g (5 oz) bulgur
5 ml (1 tsp) sea salt
60 ml (4 tbsp) tahini
25 ml (5 tsp) lemon juice
60 g (2 oz) toasted sunflower seeds or
chopped, toasted almonds
6 eggs

First, put lentils into small saucepan with 400 ml (14 fl oz) water, the 2.5 ml (1/2 tsp) sea salt and turmeric and cook gently until soft and liquid is absorbed. Drain.

Heat sunflower oil in a large frying pan with a lid. Add spring onions, garlic and pepper and sauté until soft. Add the spices and toss over low heat for a minute or two. Add bulgur and toss until coated, then add another 5 ml (1 tsp) sea salt.

Mix 500 ml (17 fl oz) boiling water with tahini and lemon juice. (Don't be concerned if the tahini melts into threads.) Stir into mixture in pan, then cover tightly and cook on low heat for 5 minutes. Turn off heat and leave for another 5 minutes. Use a fork to mix in the lentils and sunflower seeds or almonds, tossing lightly until thoroughly combined, then turn on to a large heated platter and keep warm, covered, in a low oven until ready to serve.

Fry the eggs. As soon as they're ready, arrange them on top of the pilaff and serve immediately. If using hard-boiled eggs, first moisten the pilaff by forking in a lump of butter, top with eggs and serve with a bowl of chutney.
*Serves 6.*

---

# MILLET PILAFF WITH EGGS FLORENTINE

*Although these are two completely separate dishes, they make such a good combination that I am featuring them as one meal. The eggs, baked on a bed of spinach in individual ramekins, are served to one side of the dinner plate, with a mound of the nutty pilaff alongside. This method of presentation makes a nice change, and only a fork is used to dip into the two. The result is a super combination of flavours and textures, but the pilaff can, of course, be served elsewhere as a particularly wholesome alternative to rice. Start with the baked eggs Florentine as the cooking time is slightly longer than for the millet. Cook the pilaff while the eggs are baking. For added flavour, the millet should be pre-toasted. Do this by spreading it out on a baking tray and placing in a moderate oven until a light golden brown.*

## BAKED EGGS FLORENTINE

500 g (18 oz) frozen spinach, thawed
sea salt and a little freshly
grated nutmeg
8 eggs
200 ml (7 fl oz) soured cream
sea salt and paprika

Cook the thawed spinach in a little water. Drain, if necessary, and then season with sea salt and nutmeg. Divide the spinach between eight small ramekins, lightly greased with butter. Break an egg into each ramekin and over each egg spoon 25 ml (5 tsp) soured cream. Dust with a little sea salt and paprika, and then arrange ramekins, not touching, in a large roasting tin, one-third filled with water. Bake at 180°C (350°F, gas 4) for about 45 minutes or until set.

---

## NUTTY MILLET PILAFF

25 ml (5 tsp) sunflower oil
30 g (1 oz) butter
1 bunch spring onions, chopped
1 large red pepper, seeded
and finely diced
200 g (7 oz) de-husked millet, toasted
5 ml (1 tsp) sea salt
100 ml (7 tbsp) chopped parsley
125 g (4 oz) lentil sprouts
60 g (2 oz) toasted sunflower seeds
a nut or two of butter (optional)

Heat oil and butter in wide, heavy-based frying pan with a lid. Add spring onions and red pepper and allow to soften over medium heat. Add millet and toss until coated. Add 750 ml (1¼ pints) boiling water, the sea salt and parsley, stir to mix, then cover and simmer very gently for 25-30 minutes, until millet is tender and liquid absorbed. (Don't make it stodgy by stirring.) Fork in the lentil sprouts and sunflower seeds and, if liked, a nut or two of butter.
*Serves 6 — presuming that some diners will have 2 eggs and some will have 1.*

*Oriental Rice (p. 45) and Vegetable Biryani (p. 48) with cucumber and soured cream salad.*

# VEGETABLE BIRYANI

*Based on a dish from Northern India, this is an aromatic combination of rice, lentils, vegetables and spices. The dish has only a gentle bite, but the amount of masala used may be increased to taste. A cooling cucumber, mint and sour cream salad makes a fine accompaniment.*
*See p. 62 for another version of biryani.*

**200 g (7 oz) brown rice**
**100 g (3½ oz) brown lentils, picked over and rinsed**
**5 ml (1 tsp) each sea salt, turmeric and ground coriander**
**2.5 ml (½ tsp) ground cumin**
**1 stick cinnamon**
**200 g (7 oz) aubergine, washed and cubed**
**60 g (2 oz) butter**
**25 ml (5 tsp) sunflower oil**
**2 leeks, sliced**
**1 large onion, chopped**
**2-4 cloves garlic, crushed**
**2.5 ml (½ tsp) pure roasted masala or more to taste**
**1 red pepper, seeded and diced**
**4 juicy tomatoes, skinned and chopped**
**300 g (11 oz) small baby marrows, pared and sliced**
**150 g (5 oz) green peas**
**a pinch each of sea salt and sugar**
**60 g (2 oz) slivered almonds**
**90 g (3 oz) sultanas**

Put rice, lentils, salt, spices and 800 ml (27 fl oz) water into a saucepan. Bring to the boil, cover, lower heat and leave to cook gently for about 50 minutes, by which time liquid should be absorbed. Fluff up with a fork and remove cinnamon stick.

Meanwhile, dégorge aubergine. Heat 30 g (1 oz) butter and oil in a large frying pan and sauté leeks, onion, garlic and masala. When softened, add the aubergine, red pepper, tomatoes, baby marrows and peas. Cook for about 10 minutes, stirring occasionally, until marrows are translucent. Remove from stove and add salt and sugar.

In a large, deep, buttered dish, layer one third of rice, half the vegetable mixture, another third of the rice, the remaining vegetable mixture, then remainder of the rice. Bake, covered, at 160°C (325°F, gas 3) for 30 minutes. Just before end of baking time, fry almonds in butter. When lightly browned, add sultanas, heat through and spoon over top of biryani.
*Serves about 8.*

# WILD RICE WITH WATER CHESTNUTS

*Wild rice is the seed of a grass which grows in the shallow waters of lakes and waterways in parts of North America. Because of the locality, these slim, blackish seeds with their distinctive, nutty flavour are difficult to harvest, so they are wildly expensive and best used with other types of rice. There are different ways of cooking wild rice, but it may be cooked together with brown rice. The following dish is a lovely combination of flavours and textures, and delicious served with large, grilled mushrooms. Not an economical family meal, but an excellent choice for a special occasion.*

**100 g (3½ oz) wild rice, rinsed**
**100 g (3½ oz) brown rice**
**30 g (1 oz) butter**
**25 ml (5 tsp) sunflower oil**
**2 medium onions, sliced into thin rings**
**60 g (2 oz) slivered almonds**
**2 cloves garlic, crushed**
**1 red pepper, seeded and diced**
**1 large stick celery, plus leaves, chopped**
**1 small knob root ginger, peeled and grated**
**3 rings fresh pineapple, diced**
**125 g (4 oz) canned water chestnuts, drained and sliced**
**25 ml (5 tsp) soy sauce**
**10 ml (2 tsp) honey**
**60 g (2 oz) lentil sprouts**

Bring 600 ml (1 pint) salted water to boil in a heavy saucepan. Add wild rice, brown rice and a dash of oil, stir once to mix, and as soon as water returns to the boil, reduce heat to very low, cover and leave to simmer for 50-60 minutes, until tender and all water has been absorbed.

Meanwhile, heat half the butter and oil in a large frying pan. Add one of the onions and the almonds, and toss over medium heat until browned. Remove from pan and set aside. Add remaining butter and oil to pan and sauté the other onion, garlic, red pepper, celery and ginger. When softening, stir in pineapple, water chestnuts, soy sauce, 45 ml (3 tbsp) water and honey. Cover and simmer on a very low heat for 10 minutes. Fork in cooked rice and lentil sprouts. Check seasoning — a little more soy sauce may be necessary — then turn mixture, which should be moist and shiny, on to large heated platter. Top with reserved onion and almonds, and serve at once.
*Serves 4–6.*

# NUTTY VEGETABLE RICE WITH STUFFED MUSHROOMS

*A marvellous dinner dish, smart enough for entertaining and a top favourite in our house. Cooked rice is tossed with sautéed vegetables and nuts; big brown mushrooms are baked separately. Together they make a superb combination of textures and flavours.*

### MUSHROOMS
**8 large brown mushrooms, wiped**
**4 spring onions, chopped**
**60 g (2 oz) stale, finely crumbed brown or wholewheat breadcrumbs**
**12 needles fresh rosemary, finely chopped**
**30-45 ml (2-3 tbsp) thick mayonnaise**
**a pinch of sea salt and milled black pepper to taste**
**sliced mozzarella or grated low-fat Gouda or Cheddar cheese**
**45 g (1½ oz) garlic butter**

### RICE
**45 ml (3 tbsp) sunflower oil**
**2 leeks, sliced**
**1 onion, chopped**
**2 sticks celery, plus a few leaves, chopped**
**1 red or yellow pepper, seeded and diced**
**100 ml (7 tbsp) toasted sunflower seeds or 75 g (2½ oz) coarsely chopped pecan nuts**
**100 ml (7 tbsp) chopped parsley**
**325 g (12 oz) cooked brown rice**
**30 ml (2 tbsp) soy sauce**

Remove stalks and a little of the centre of each mushroom. Chop finely and mix with onions, breadcrumbs, rosemary, just enough mayonnaise to moisten, and salt. Lightly oil base of large baking dish and arrange mushrooms in it, hollows up. Season. Fill each mushroom with a spoon of the stuffing, then top with cheese. Put a small lump of garlic butter on each and bake at 180°C (350°F, gas 4) for about 25 minutes until tender and cheese has melted.

Meanwhile, heat oil and soften leeks and onion. Add celery and diced pepper and stir-fry over low heat until just tender. Fork in remaining ingredients for rice mixture. Heat through on very low heat.

Spoon the rice into warmed serving dish. Top each serving of rice with two of the mushrooms, spooning the juices over.
*Serves 4.*

# COUSCOUS WITH CHICKPEA AND VEGETABLE STEW

*The following is a fuss-free and quick way of preparing couscous. Do not prepare in advance as it easily becomes stodgy. The accompanying stew is thick with vegetables, chickpeas and tahini, making this a dish for those initiated into foreign flavours.*

### STEW
30 ml (2 tbsp) sunflower oil
15 g (½ oz) butter
1 large onion, chopped
2 cloves garlic, crushed
1 green pepper, seeded and diced
2.5 ml (½ tsp) ground cumin
5 ml (1 tsp) ground coriander
425 g (15 oz) butternut squash, cubed
200 g (7 oz) cauliflower florets
90 g (3 oz) shredded spinach leaves
12 baby potatoes, scrubbed
4 carrots, julienned
325 g (12 oz) cooked chickpeas
2 sticks cinnamon
2 bay leaves
5 ml (1 tsp) each sea salt and
light brown sugar
500 ml (17 fl oz) vegetable stock or
liquid from cooking chickpeas
10-15 ml (2-3 tsp) tahini

### COUSCOUS
175 g (6 oz) refined semolina couscous
2.5 ml (½ tsp) turmeric
5 ml (1 tsp) sea salt
a nut of butter

Heat the oil and butter in a large saucepan. Add the onion, garlic and green pepper and sauté until softening. Mix in all the spices and toss for 1-2 minutes. Add all the vegetables and toss until well mixed, then add the remaining ingredients for stew, except tahini. Bring to the boil, then cover and simmer on low heat, stirring occasionally, until the vegetables are cooked and the sauce is thick. Remove cinnamon and bay leaves, and stir in the tahini.

Prepare the couscous by putting it into a saucepan with 500 ml (17 fl oz) water, turmeric and the sea salt. Bring to the boil, stir, then cover and remove from heat. Leave it to stand for 10 minutes, then lightly fork in the nut of butter.

To serve, spread couscous around the edge of a large, warmed platter and pile the stew in the middle.
*Serves 4–6.*

# MUSHROOM RICE WITH LENTIL SPROUTS AND TAHINI

*This dish affords a gentle introduction to the use of tahini. Mixed with lemon juice and water, it adds a creamy texture and a slightly smoky flavour to the combination of rice, vegetables, lentil sprouts and sunflower seeds.*

### SAUCE
100 ml (7 tbsp) tahini
45 ml (3 tbsp) lemon juice
100 ml (7 tbsp) cold water

### RICE
60 ml (4 tbsp) sunflower oil
2 leeks, sliced
1 small onion, chopped
2 cloves garlic, crushed
1 green, red or yellow pepper,
seeded and diced
2 sticks celery, sliced
250 g (9 oz) brown mushrooms,
wiped and sliced
45 ml (3 tbsp) soy sauce
a pinch of sugar
100 ml (7 tbsp) chopped parsley
475 g (17 oz) cooked brown rice
90 g (3 oz) lentil sprouts
60 g (2 oz) toasted sunflower seeds
feta cheese, rinsed and crumbled
for topping

Stir tahini very well before using, or turn into a small bowl and whisk thoroughly. Slowly stir in lemon juice — the mixture will become thick and grainy. Add water gradually, stirring the sauce until it is smooth and creamy.

Heat oil in a large pan and soften leeks, onion and garlic. Add pepper and celery and stir-fry over low heat for a few minutes. Add mushrooms and when softening, add soy sauce, sugar and parsley. Cover and keep on very low heat for about 10 minutes until juices form, then fork in remaining ingredients. The mixture should be moist and glistening. No salt should be necessary due to the generous amount of soy sauce.

Stir in tahini sauce and heat without boiling. Turn into warmed serving dish, top with feta and place in moderate oven briefly just to heat through.
*Serves 6.*

# PULSES

## SPICED CHICKPEAS

*A fragrant stew to serve on brown rice with
bowls of coconut and chopped nuts
and a green salad.*

45 ml (3 tbsp) sunflower oil
2 onions, chopped
2-3 cloves garlic, crushed
2.5 ml (½ tsp) each ground cumin,
turmeric, cinnamon and ginger
5 ml (1 tsp) ground coriander
2 sticks celery, chopped
1 green pepper, seeded and diced
550 g (19 oz) cooked chickpeas, drained
15 g (½ oz) chopped parsley
400 g (14 oz) canned tomatoes,
chopped, plus juice
2 bay leaves
250 ml (8 fl oz) water or vegetable stock
5 ml (1 tsp) sea salt or 10 ml (2 tsp)
vegetable salt
5 ml (1 tsp) sugar

Heat oil in a large saucepan. Add onions,
garlic, spices, celery and green pepper.
Cover and cook over very low heat until the
onions are soft. Add remaining ingredients,
bring to the boil, then cover and simmer on
low heat for about 30 minutes, stirring occasionally. Add a little water if necessary, for
a good consistency. Check seasoning, and
serve as suggested.
*Serves 4–6.*

*Mediterranean Chickpea Casserole (p. 53).*

51

# CHICKPEA STEW WITH TAHINI SAUCE

*If you like tahini, you'll love this chickpea dish, subtly flavoured with ginger and cumin. Spooned over brown rice, it could be classed as a major protein meal. Although the stew does contain vegetables, a crisp green salad just ties it all together. Remember to save the cooking liquid when draining chickpeas, as it is added to the dish.*

45 ml (3 tbsp) sunflower oil
2 onions, chopped
3 leeks, thinly sliced
4 sticks celery, thinly sliced
3 cloves garlic, crushed
6 medium baby marrows, pared and julienned
5 ml (1 tsp) each ground cumin and ginger
30 ml (2 tbsp) brown flour
1 kg (2¼ lb) cooked chickpeas
750 ml (1¼ pints) liquid from cooking chickpeas
75-100 ml (5-7 tbsp) tahini
45 ml (3 tbsp) soy sauce (a little less if liquid is salty

Heat oil in a large pan. Add onions, leeks, celery, garlic and baby marrows. Mix well, then allow them to sweat over a low heat, half-covered, until nearly soft. Mix in the spices (for a fairly 'hot' flavour, double quantities of both spices) and cook for a further 2 minutes. Mix in the flour, then add chickpeas. Stir the cooking liquid with the tahini and soy sauce. Add to stew, bring to the boil slowly, cover and simmer gently for about 15 minutes before serving. It may also be cooled and reheated.
*Serves 8.*

# BUTTER BEAN, MUSHROOM AND WALNUT CURRY

*This easy dish, with its rather surprising combination of ingredients, is high on my list of favourites. Nourishing and quick to make, it has a rich caramel colour and a lovely tang. Ladle servings over brown rice and hand bowls of coconut, chutney and a green salad.*

45 ml (3 tbsp) sunflower oil
1 large onion, finely chopped
1 large Golden Delicious apple, peeled and diced
10 ml (2 tsp) curry powder
5 ml (1 tsp) ground coriander
2.5 ml (½ tsp) each turmeric and ground cumin and cinnamon
45 ml (3 tbsp) brown flour
250 ml (8 fl oz) vegetable stock or water
250 ml (8 fl oz) milk
5 ml (1 tsp) sea salt
25 ml (5 tsp) tomato purée
a pinch of sugar
30 g (1 oz) butter
250 g (9 oz) brown mushrooms, wiped and sliced
1 red pepper, seeded and diced
60 g (2 oz) coarsely chopped walnuts
400 g (14 oz) canned choice grade butter beans, drained

Heat oil and lightly fry onion and apple. Add spices and allow to sizzle gently for about 2 minutes. Sprinkle in flour, then slowly stir in stock or water and milk. When thickening, add salt, tomato purée and sugar. Cover and simmer very gently for 20 minutes, stirring occasionally to prevent sticking. Meanwhile, heat butter in separate pan. Add mushrooms, red pepper and walnuts and fry until mushrooms are just softening. Stir into curry sauce, add beans, then simmer on low heat until very hot. Check seasoning (if water has been used, you may need to add a little salt).
*Serves 4–5.*

# CHICKPEAS AND BROCCOLI IN MUSTARD SAUCE

*A simple but tasty combination of chickpeas and vegetables in a creamy sauce. Serve on brown rice or pasta and top with grated Cheddar or crumbled feta cheese, or with baked potatoes and cottage cheese.*

500 g (18 oz) broccoli
60 ml (4 tbsp) sunflower oil
3 leeks, thinly sliced
1 small onion, chopped
2 cloves garlic, crushed
400 ml (14 fl oz) liquid from cooking chickpeas or vegetable stock
5 ml (1 tsp) sea salt and milled black pepper to taste
75 ml (5 tbsp) brown flour
375 ml (12 fl oz) milk
725 g (1 lb 7 oz) cooked chickpeas
15 ml (1 tbsp) Dijon mustard
15 ml (1 tbsp) lemon juice
75 ml (5 tbsp) double cream or soured cream

Prepare broccoli: remove only the tips of the stalks, chop remainder of stalks thinly and the florets fairly coarsely.

Heat sunflower oil in a large pan. Add leeks, onion and garlic and sweat over low heat, shaking pan occasionally. Add the prepared broccoli, 200 ml (7 fl oz) of the liquid and seasoning. Cover and cook gently until soft. Sprinkle in the flour and toss to mix, then slowly stir in remaining liquid and the milk. Stir over low heat until the sauce has thickened, then add remaining ingredients. Heat through, stirring, and allow mixture to bubble gently for a few minutes to blend flavours. Check seasoning and serve at once.
*Serves 6–8.*

---

## BEURRE MANIÉ

This is a paste made of butter and flour, which is kneaded together until smooth, and used for enriching and thickening sauces and stews. It should be whisked, a little at a time, into the hot liquid, which is then slowly brought back to the boil. The classic ratio of butter to flour is 3:2, but less butter may be used with good results.

---

# CHICKPEA STEW

*Serve on brown rice and top with grated cheese.*

30 g (1 oz) butter
25 ml (5 tsp) sunflower oil
1 large onion, chopped
2 cloves garlic, crushed
2 carrots, diced
1 red pepper, seeded and diced
250 g (9 oz) brown mushrooms, wiped and sliced
250 g (9 oz) tomatoes, skinned and chopped
25 ml (5 tsp) tomato purée
15 g (½ oz) chopped parsley
2.5 ml (½ tsp) each dried basil and thyme
725 g (1 lb 7 oz) cooked chickpeas
125 ml (4 fl oz) vegetable stock
sea salt and milled black pepper to taste

Heat butter and oil in large saucepan. Stir-fry onion, garlic, carrots, red pepper and mushrooms. Add remaining ingredients. Season, cover and simmer for 30 minutes. Thicken sauce with beurre manié.
*Serves 5–6.*

# MEDITERRANEAN CHICKPEA CASSEROLE

*An aromatic, spicy combination of vegetables and chickpeas, slowly simmered together to make a marvellous topping for brown rice or pasta. This dish may be made in advance and reheated, and is even good cold.*

45 ml (3 tbsp) olive oil
25 ml (5 tsp) sunflower oil
2 large onions, chopped
2 cloves garlic, crushed
10 ml (2 tsp) ground coriander
5 ml (1 tsp) each ground cinnamon and cumin
500 g (18 oz) aubergines, cubed and dégorged
2 carrots, diced
400 g (14 oz) ripe tomatoes, skinned and chopped
725 g (1 lb 7 oz) cooked chickpeas
5 ml (1 tsp) sea salt and milled black pepper to taste
5 ml (1 tsp) sugar
2 bay leaves
15 g (½ oz) chopped parsley
500 ml (17 fl oz) vegetable stock or water or liquid from drained chickpeas
black olives (optional)
feta cheese, rinsed and crumbled for topping

Heat both oils in large saucepan. Add onions and garlic, and when translucent add spices and cook for 1 minute. Add aubergines and carrots and toss, over low heat, until coated. Add remaining ingredients, except olives and feta, bring to the boil, then cover and simmer over very low heat for 45-60 minutes, stirring occasionally. When ready, mixture should be thick, like a stew, but if it needs binding, stir in a little flour slaked with water. Remove bay leaves and check seasoning. If cooking in advance, transfer to suitable container and cool. Reheat gently before serving, adding a little water or stock if necessary. Stir in a few olives, if using, and spoon into large, warmed serving dish. Top with feta.
*Serves 6.*

---

## SPICED MIXED RICE AND LENTILS

As this useful recipe combines a pulse and grain, it is more nutritious than serving just one or the other, and its delightful flavour marries perfectly with curries, or bean or chickpea casseroles. Or toss it with French dressing and serve cold, as a salad.

200 g (7 oz) each brown rice and brown lentils, picked over and rinsed
1.1 litres (2 pints) water
5 ml (1 tsp) sea salt
4 star anise
2 sticks cinnamon
2 bay leaves
6 white cardamom pods
5 ml (1 tsp) each ground cumin, ground coriander and turmeric
45 ml (3 tbsp) dried onion flakes
a nut of butter

Put all ingredients, except butter, in a saucepan. Bring to the boil, cover and simmer on lowest heat for about 1 hour until liquid is absorbed. Remove spices and bay leaves, and fork in butter.
*Serves 8.*

---

*Overleaf: Mushroom and Lentil Moussaka (p. 57), Quick Butter Bean and Mushroom Goulash (p. 56) and Pot Beans (p. 65).*

## VEGETABLE AND BUTTER BEAN HURRY CURRY

*There's no denying that many meatless meals are hard on the cook. Pulses take time to soak and cook; vegetables need cleaning and chopping. There's also no denying that these freshly prepared ingredients taste the best. But sometimes a cook simply has to cheat. This recipe is not gourmet fare, but it is both tasty and filling.*

45 ml (3 tbsp) sunflower oil
2 large onions, chopped
2-4 cloves garlic, crushed
30 ml (2 tbsp) curry powder,
or more to taste
5 ml (1 tsp) turmeric
1 kg (2¼ lb) frozen vegetables (e.g. marrows, carrots, cauliflower and peas)
500 g (18 oz) ripe tomatoes, skinned and chopped into small pieces
500 ml (17 fl oz) vegetable stock or water
5 ml (1 tsp) sea salt
45 ml (3 tbsp) chutney
25 ml (5 tsp) tomato purée
2 bay leaves
2 × 400 g (14 oz) cans choice grade butter beans, drained
a little lemon juice
45 g (1½ oz) desiccated coconut

Heat oil and soften onions and garlic. Add curry powder and turmeric and sizzle for a minute or two. Add just-thawed vegetables and toss to coat. Add tomatoes, stock or water, salt, chutney, tomato purée and bay leaves. Cover and simmer gently for 15 minutes. Add beans, lemon juice and coconut and heat through. Add a little extra liquid if needed. If time allows, transfer to suitable container and cool for flavour to develop. Remove bay leaves and reheat gently. Check seasoning and serve on brown rice with sambals.
*Serves 8.*

> To me, one of the very nicest meals is one that is so simple that no recipe is required. We love it — particularly on those evenings when I just do not wish to be in the kitchen. Young potatoes, scrubbed and steamed (not baked) are served with fried mushrooms (sometimes I add spinach), cottage cheese and soured cream. It's a surprisingly addictive combination.

## BOSTON BAKED BUTTER BEANS

*This is a tasty but totally unpretentious meal. Based on an old-fashioned American dish, my recipe includes the traditional mustard, molasses and spices, but without the fat salt belly pork which is normally added. I have also shortened the cooking time considerably — traditionally (with the pork) it is cooked for about 8 hours! The following quantities can easily be halved. It is astonishingly economical. The dish is perfectly rounded off with the addition of brown rice or baked potatoes, grated Cheddar or cottage cheese and a cabbage, carrot and pineapple slaw. It also reheats well. (See box on p. 64.)*

500 g (18 oz) butter beans
100 ml (7 tbsp) sunflower oil
4 large onions, chopped
4 sticks celery, plus some leaves, chopped
6 medium carrots, diced into small cubes
4 bay leaves
20 g (¾ oz) chopped parsley
20 ml (4 tsp) mustard powder
20 ml (4 tsp) light brown sugar
45 ml (3 tbsp) molasses
500 ml (17 fl oz) tomato passata
10 ml (2 tsp) ground mixed spice
500 ml (17 fl oz) vegetable stock or water
5 ml (1 tsp) sea salt
20 ml (4 tsp) Worcestershire sauce

Soak beans overnight, drain and rinse and put into a large saucepan. Cover with cold water, bring to the boil, boil rapidly for 10 minutes, then simmer gently until nearly tender — about 45 minutes — adding salt towards the end. Drain.

Heat oil in a large saucepan, add onions, celery and carrots and sweat over low heat until onion is glossy and carrots are tender. Mix in remaining ingredients, except beans, then turn into a large baking dish. Stir in the beans, then cover and bake at 140°C (275°F, gas 1) for 1 hour. Stir to mix, adding extra liquid if necessary, then return to oven and bake for another 1¼ hours.

Remove bay leaves before serving. If making ahead, you will probably need to add a little extra stock or water before reheating, to ensure a juicy mixture.*
*Serves 10–12.*

* If preferred, this dish may be cooked on top of the stove. Cover and simmer very gently until beans are tender and flavour has developed, checking occasionally to see if extra liquid is needed.

## QUICK BUTTER BEAN AND MUSHROOM GOULASH

*Good quality canned butter beans are a useful time-saver and can be used to pad out many a dish. The following is a tasty, simple and quickly prepared example.*

30 ml (2 tbsp) sunflower oil
1 large onion, chopped
250 g (9 oz) white or brown mushrooms, wiped and sliced
2 sticks celery, sliced
1 green or red pepper, seeded and diced
7.5 ml (1½ tsp) paprika
30 ml (2 tbsp) brown flour
125 ml (4 fl oz) tomato passata
2.5 ml (½ tsp) sea salt and milled black pepper to taste
2 × 400 g (14 oz) cans butter beans, drained
125 ml (4 fl oz) soured cream
grated Cheddar cheese for topping

Heat oil and fry onion lightly. Add mushrooms, celery and pepper and toss over medium heat until softening. Sprinkle in paprika and flour and toss to mix. Add tomato passata, 250 ml (8 fl oz) water, seasoning and beans. Cover and simmer very gently for 15 minutes, stirring once or twice to prevent mixture from sticking to the bottom of the pan as it thickens, but taking care not to mash the beans.

If possible, set aside to cool for a while (see box on p. 64), then reheat gently, swirling in the soured cream. Check seasoning and serve topped with Cheddar cheese.
*Serves 5–6*

> ### BUTTER BEANS
> —— • ——
> Also called lima or large kidney beans, these are big, flat, white and relatively quick to cook (about 50 minutes of simmering), although they do need overnight soaking.
>
> Canned butter beans are convenient and inexpensive, and unlike some haricot beans, are not mixed with tomato sauce. This is a real bonus and increases their versatility in both salads and cooked dishes.

# MUSHROOM AND LENTIL MOUSSAKA

*As with all moussakas, this dish takes time to prepare, but makes a delicious and nourishing meal served with a crisp salad and hot garlic bread. The dish reheats very well at 160°C (325°F, gas 3) for 30 minutes.*

575 g (1¼ lb) aubergines
sunflower oil for frying
200 g (7 oz) brown lentils, picked over and rinsed
25 ml (5 tsp) olive oil
1 large onion, chopped
1 green pepper, seeded and diced
2 cloves garlic, crushed
250 g (9 oz) brown mushrooms, wiped and sliced
400 g (14 oz) tomatoes, skinned and chopped
10 ml (2 tsp) brown sugar
2.5 ml (½ tsp) ground cinnamon
1 bay leaf
2.5 ml (½ tsp) sea salt
100 ml (7 tbsp) chopped parsley

TOPPING
45 g (1½ oz) butter
45 ml (3 tbsp) brown flour
500 ml (17 fl oz) milk (full-cream or semi-skimmed)
2 eggs, separated
sea salt and milled black pepper to taste
2.5 ml (½ tsp) freshly grated nutmeg
175 g (6 oz) grated Cheddar cheese

Cut stem ends off aubergines, slice into 5-mm (¼-in) thick rings, then dégorge. Fry on both sides until lightly browned and soft. If fried on a fairly low heat in a heavy-based pan and half-covered every now and then, much less oil will be absorbed.

Meanwhile, boil lentils in 500 ml (17 fl oz) salted water for 50 minutes or until soft and the water is absorbed.

In a large frying pan, heat the olive oil and soften the onion, green pepper and garlic. Add the mushrooms and when softened, add the tomatoes, sugar, cinnamon, bay leaf, salt and parsley. Cover and simmer for 20 minutes, stirring occasionally. Remove the bay leaf and stir in the cooked lentils. The mixture should be moist and fairly thick.

Make topping by melting the butter, then stirring in the flour. Cook for 1 minute, remove from heat and slowly stir in the milk. Return to heat and cook, stirring, until thickened. Beat the egg yolks with a little hot sauce and then mix in with the sauce, using a balloon whisk. Season with salt, pepper and nutmeg. Stiffly whisk the egg whites and fold in.

To assemble, cover the base of a 30 × 20-cm (12 × 8-in) baking dish with half the aubergine slices, then spoon the lentil mixture over. Cover with the remaining aubergine slices, then pour the topping over. Sprinkle with grated Cheddar cheese and bake at 180°C (350°F, gas 4) for 30 minutes, then turn off the oven and leave for 15 minutes to settle.
*Serves 6.*

# SPICY LENTIL AND MUSHROOM STEW

*A dish with an intriguing flavour; no one ever seems able to guess what all the ingredients are. Economical, easily prepared and excellent served on brown rice or pasta. Serve with additional coconut, chutney and a bowl of yoghurt with cucumber and chopped fresh coriander.*

60 ml (4 tbsp) sunflower oil
1 large onion, chopped
2 leeks, sliced
2 cloves garlic, crushed
1 green pepper, seeded and diced
15 ml (1 tbsp) curry powder
5 ml (1 tsp) ground coriander
2 sticks cinnamon
4 whole cloves
250 g (9 oz) brown mushrooms, wiped and chopped
2-3 carrots, julienned
300 g (11 oz) brown lentils, picked over and rinsed
1 litre (1¾ pints) vegetable stock or water
25 ml (5 tsp) tomato purée
10 ml (2 tsp) sea salt
5 ml (1 tsp) honey
60 ml (4 tbsp) each desiccated coconut and soured cream (optional)
6 hard-boiled eggs, quartered

Heat oil in a large pan. Add onion, leeks, garlic and green pepper and stir-fry over medium heat until softening. Add all the spices and toss for a minute or two. Add mushrooms and carrots and toss until combined with vegetables and spices. Add lentils, stock or water, tomato purée, salt and honey. Bring to the boil, then cover and simmer on lowest heat for about 1 hour, stirring occasionally. At end of cooking period lentils should be soft and most of liquid absorbed. If possible, leave to cool in suitable container. To reheat, remove cinnamon and cloves, if you can find them, and add a little more water, as the mixture absorbs excess liquid on standing and although the stew should not be watery it should not be too thick or dry either. Stir in coconut and swirl in cream, if using, and reheat gently. Pile on to warmed serving platter and surround with eggs.
*Serves 6–8.*

*Overleaf: Lentil Dahl with Eggs and Masala Sauce (p. 60) and Vegetarian Bobotie (p. 69), served with poppadums.*

# LENTIL DAHL
# WITH EGGS
# AND MASALA SAUCE

*This is a bright and beautiful dish, consisting of a spicy purée of red lentils, topped with hard-boiled eggs and a sauce lightly spiked with masala. When baked, it looks rather like a golden brown soufflé. Serve with Basmati rice, bowls of coconut and chutney and a green salad. If you have rocket in your garden, add a few chopped leaves.*

300 g (11 oz) red lentils, picked over
and rinsed
1 onion, finely chopped
2 cloves garlic, crushed
5 ml (1 tsp) each turmeric and
ground cumin
10 ml (2 tsp) ground coriander
1 stick cinnamon
2 bay leaves
3 whole cloves
5 ml (1 tsp) sea salt
6 eggs, hard-boiled and halved
paprika

SAUCE
15 ml (1 tbsp) sunflower oil
15 g (½ oz) butter
1 onion, finely chopped
45 ml (3 tbsp) brown flour
5 ml (1 tsp) leaf masala (or more to taste)
250 ml (8 fl oz) vegetable stock or water
250 ml (8 fl oz) milk
25 ml (5 tsp) chutney
5 ml (1 tsp) lemon juice
2.5 ml (½ tsp) sea salt

Put lentils, onion, garlic, spices, salt and 750 ml (1¼ pints) water into a saucepan. Stir to mix, bring to the boil, then cover and simmer on lowest heat for 20 minutes, stirring once. Red lentils soften quickly, and when done, the mixture will be mushy and moist. Remove cinnamon, bay leaves and cloves, if you can find them, and spread evenly into a lightly oiled baking dish — a deep, 23-cm (9-in) pie dish is just right.

Make the sauce: heat sunflower oil and butter in a heavy-based saucepan and braise onion. Stir in flour and masala and cook gently for about 2 minutes. Slowly add the stock or water and milk, stirring until thickened. Add the chutney, lemon juice and sea salt. Half-cover the pan and simmer the sauce on low heat for about 20 minutes, stirring occasionally.

Arrange eggs, rounded sides up, on top of lentil mixture. Strain sauce through a fine sieve and pour over — it will coat the eggs and it should cover the lentil mixture completely. Dust with paprika. If working ahead, set aside at this stage. Bake at 160°C (325°F, gas 3) for about 40 minutes or until just bubbling.
*Serves 4.*

---

### SHERRY
·

Cheap and sweet is fine to use in cooking. A touch of sweetness brings out the flavour in savoury foods, and it is especially useful in reducing the saltiness of soy sauce.

---

# SPICY
# STOVE-TOP BEANS

*An economical and easily prepared meal, using basic ingredients and canned beans. The result is a thick, bright and flavoursome stew to serve on rice. Serve with bowls of chutney, coconut and sliced bananas or a cucumber raita.*

30 ml (2 tbsp) sunflower oil
1 large onion, chopped
1-2 cloves garlic, crushed
1 large green pepper, seeded and diced
5-10 ml (1-2 tsp) curry powder
5 ml (1 tsp) ground coriander
2.5 ml (½ tsp) each ground fennel
and cumin
2 sticks cinnamon
2 bay leaves
2 × 425 g (15 oz) cans choice grade baked
beans in tomato, undrained
1 Golden Delicious apple, peeled and
finely diced
45 g (1½ oz) seedless raisins or sultanas
25 ml (5 tsp) chutney
20 ml (4 tsp) lemon juice
at least 125 ml (4 fl oz) water

Heat the sunflower oil and sauté the onion, garlic and green pepper. Add the spices and toss over low heat for 2 minutes, then add the remining ingredients. Mix well, then bring to the boil, cover, and simmer very gently for 30 minutes, stirring occasionally to prevent sticking, and adding more water if mixture becomes too thick. When stirring, take care not to mash beans. Check seasoning, remove bay leaves and cinnamon sticks, and serve as suggested.
*Serves 6.*

---

# SPICED LENTILS AND
# MUSHROOMS
# WITH CORIANDER

*Fresh coriander puts the finishing touch to this simple but super dish. Serve on brown rice with chutney, a green salad and a loaf of hot garlic bread. On special occasions, fork a nut of butter and some toasted almond strips into the rice.*

200 g (7 oz) lentils (green or brown),
picked over and rinsed
60 ml (4 tbsp) sunflower oil
1 large onion, chopped
2 cloves garlic, crushed
5 ml (1 tsp) each ground cumin,
coriander, fennel and turmeric
250 g (9 oz) brown mushrooms,
wiped and sliced
250 g (9 oz) baby marrows, pared
and sliced
2 sticks celery, sliced
100 ml (7 tbsp) chopped parsley
500 ml (17 fl oz) vegetable or
Marmite stock
5 ml (1 tsp) sea salt and milled black
pepper to taste
desiccated coconut and fresh coriander
leaves, chopped, for topping

Cook lentils in 500 ml (17 fl oz) salted water until soft and dry — for about 50 minutes.

Heat oil and soften onion and garlic. Add spices and toss for 1-2 minutes on low heat. Add mushrooms, marrows, celery and parsley and toss until coated, then add stock and seasonings. Cover and simmer gently until vegetables are cooked — for about 20 minutes. Add cooked lentils. Mix in carefully, then simmer until mixture is hot and thick — it should be juicy and moist, not watery, but if it needs reduction, simply leave the lid off for a few minutes. Spoon into a heated serving dish and sprinkle with coconut and coriander.
*Serves 6.*

---

### VEGETABLE OR
### MARMITE STOCK
———— · ————

Home-made stock is excellent, but time-consuming. Marmite stock can often be substituted very successfully, and is ideal for vegetarian cooking as it contains no animal ingredients. Use about 5 ml (1 tsp) Marmite to 250 ml (8 fl oz) boiling water.

---

# LENTIL
AND VEGETABLE
MOUSSAKA

*Similar to Mushroom and Lentil Moussaka on
p. 57, but somewhat more Greek in character,
this recipe uses baby marrows and herbs instead
of mushrooms and introduces a different way of
preparing the aubergines. Grilled, instead of
fried, they absorb far less oil and this method
may be used for most aubergine dishes.*

45 ml (3 tbsp) sunflower oil
(or preferably half olive)
1 large onion, chopped
2 cloves garlic, crushed
200 g (7 oz) small baby marrows,
pared and sliced
1 red or yellow pepper, seeded
and sliced
4 large, juicy tomatoes, skinned
and chopped
300 g (11 oz) brown or green lentils,
picked over and rinsed
100 ml (7 tbsp) chopped parsley
5 ml (1 tsp) sea salt and milled black
pepper to taste
10 ml (2 tsp) brown sugar
2.5 ml (½ tsp) each dried basil, thyme
and oregano
750 g (1½ lb) aubergines, sliced
and dégorged
half olive, half sunflower oil for
grilling aubergines

SAUCE
45 ml (3 tbsp) sunflower oil and
a nut of butter
45 ml (3 tbsp) brown flour
500 ml (17 fl oz) milk (full-cream
or skimmed)
sea salt and milled black pepper to taste
1.25 ml (¼ tsp) grated nutmeg
175 g (6 oz) finely grated Cheddar or
low-fat cheese
2 egg yolks, beaten
4 egg whites, stiffly whisked

25 ml (5 tsp) grated Parmesan cheese
for topping

Heat the sunflower oil and lightly fry the
onion. Add garlic, marrows and pepper
and allow to soften over medium heat. Add
the tomatoes, lentils, parelsy, 750 ml (1¼
pints) water, seasoning, sugar and dried
herbs. Bring to the boil, and cover and simmer very gently for about 1 hour, stirring
occasionally. The lentils should be soft, and
the vegetable mixture thick and juicy.

Grill aubergines while vegetables are
cooking. First rinse them, then pat very dry.
I find this is most easily done by spinning
the slices in a salad spinner and then patting
dry with paper towels. Cover one very large
or two medium baking trays with a fairly
thin layer of oil — preferably half olive and
half sunflower. Arrange aubergine slices in
single layer, turning once to coat, and then
grill about 15 cm (6 in) below grill until
brown, turning once. Surprisingly, they will
not scorch as the juices are soon extracted
and they will soften at the same time as
browning.

Make sauce just before assembling. Heat
oil and butter. Add flour and cook, stirring
until nut-brown. Slowly stir in milk and
when thickened, remove from stove and
add seasoning and 100 g (3½ oz) of the
cheese. Pour a little hot sauce on to yolks,
mix and then stir into rest of sauce. Pour
into bowl and fold in stiffly whisked whites.*

To assemble, cover base of a 30 × 20-cm
(12 × 8-in) baking dish with half the aubergines. Top with half the lentil mixture.
Sprinkle with the remaining cheese. Cover
with the rest of the aubergines and spoon
over the rest of the lentil mixture, spreading
evenly. Spoon the fluffy white sauce over
the top, sprinkle with Parmesan and bake at
180°C (350°F, gas 4) for about 45 minutes
until golden brown and puffy.
*Serves 8.*

* As with all moussakas, this dish takes a
while to prepare. However, if you wish, it
may all be done in advance. In this case,
make the cheese sauce, but do not add the
egg whites. Refrigerate the sauce, then fold
in the whisked egg whites just before using.

---

### SPICES

·

When frying spices, for a curry, for
example, keep the heat low to prevent
scorching, but do allow enough time for
the flavours to be released or the finished dish won't taste as it should. With
experience, your nose will tell you when
you can start adding the rest of the
ingredients.

The best curry powders are those
that are home-made and fresh and are
made up of ground spices in varying
quantities. I don't like chillies (you will
doubtless notice their omission), but if
you like hot dishes, add ground chillies
or chilli powder to taste.

---

### PARSLEY

'Parsley is gharsley,' wrote Ogden
Nash. Nevertheless, I use it liberally; it
adds colour, flavour and vitamin C to a
dish. However, it does have quite a
strong flavour and so, unless used in a
cooked dish, remember that less is
better than more. For convenience,
wash a whole bunch, dry thoroughly in
a salad spinner, and store, unchopped,
in the refrigerator.

---

# LENTIL AND
AUBERGINE CURRY

*A simple, spicy dish which is extremely
economical, but for the almonds. Hand chutney,
coconut and a green salad.*

45 ml (3 tbsp) sunflower oil
1 large onion, chopped
2 cloves garlic, crushed
10-15 ml (2-3 tsp) curry powder
2.5 ml (½ tsp) each ground cumin,
turmeric and cinnamon
5 ml (1 tsp) each ground fennel
and coriander
300 g (11 oz) brown lentils, picked
over and rinsed
325 g (12 oz) aubergines, cubed
and dégorged
750 ml (1¼ pints) vegetable stock
or water
15 g (½ oz) chopped parsley
5 ml (1 tsp) sea salt
7.5 ml (1½ tsp) brown sugar
400 g (14 oz) canned tomatoes
with onions
toasted almond strips

Heat oil in large saucepan, add onion and
fry lightly. Add garlic and all the spices and
stir over low heat for a minute or two. Add
rest of ingredients, except almonds. Stir to
mix, then cover and simmer gently for 50-60
minutes, stirring occasionally. Add extra
liquid now and then to ensure a good sauce
— the mixture should not become too thick
or dry. When ready, remove from heat and
allow to cool in suitable container, if time
allows, for flavours to blend. Reheat gently
until piping hot, and serve on brown rice or
pasta. Top each serving with toasted almonds, for a delicious flavour and crunch.
*Serves 6.*

# BIRYANI

*This version is layered with hard-boiled eggs instead of vegetables. (See p. 48 for a biryani recipe with vegetables.) Once again, the spicy flavour is very subtle because this is my preference, but if you like stronger flavours, increase the quantities of spices. It may be assembled in advance and baked when wanted. Serve with bowls of chutney, coconut, sliced bananas, thick yoghurt and a tomato and onion salad. This dish is even good served cold.*

200 g (7 oz) brown rice
5 ml (1 tsp) turmeric
200 g (7 oz) brown or green lentils, picked over and rinsed
vegetable stock or water
45 ml (3 tbsp) sunflower oil
2 large onions, sliced into thin rings
2 cloves garlic, crushed
2 fat sticks cinnamon
4 whole cloves
5 ml (1 tsp) each ground fennel, cumin and coriander
6 eggs, hard-boiled and sliced into rings
30-45 g (1-1¹/₂ oz) butter, slivered

GARNISH
15 ml (1 tbsp) sunflower oil
2.5 ml (¹/₂ tsp) masala
100 ml (7 tbsp) slivered almonds
75 g (2¹/₂ oz) seedless raisins

Parboil the rice in 550 ml (18 fl oz) salted water with turmeric for 30 minutes. Parboil the lentils in 500 ml (17 fl oz) salted water. In both cases, cook over lowest heat. (The cooking process will be completed in the oven.) Drain both in a colander over a bowl and make up liquid to 500 ml (17 fl oz) with vegetable stock or water.

Heat the sunflower oil in a large pan and lightly fry the onions and garlic over medium heat until glossy and golden. Add all the spices and toss together for a few minutes until smelling delicious.

Mix together the rice, lentils and onion mixture, and spoon one-third on to base of oiled baking dish — a deep pie dish, 23-cm (9-in) diameter, is just right. Arrange half the eggs on top. Cover with another third of rice mixture, the remaining eggs and, finally, the last of the rice mixture, making sure that no cloves or cinnamon sticks lie on the top. Pour reserved liquid round the sides and dot the top with slivers of butter. If necessary, cover and set aside now. Bake, tightly covered, at 160°C (325°F, gas 3) for 50 minutes.

Meanwhile, prepare garnish by heating oil in a small pan. Keeping heat very low, add masala, almonds and raisins and toss until almonds are lightly browned and raisins plumped. Sprinkle over biryani before serving.
*Serves 6.*

# LENTIL AND TOMATO STEW

*Believe me, this easy and low-cost dish is much tastier than it sounds. It may be served on rice and sprinkled with grated cheese, or spooned into a large pie dish, covered with mashed potato and cheese and heated under the grill. Serve with a green vegetable or salad.*

300 g (11 oz) brown lentils, picked over and rinsed
5 ml (1 tsp) sea salt
45 ml (3 tbsp) sunflower oil
1 large onion, chopped
2 cloves garlic, crushed
3 medium carrots, diced
1 green pepper, seeded and diced
100 ml (7 tbsp) chopped parsley
2.5 ml (¹/₂ tsp) dried oregano
400 g (14 oz) juicy tomatoes, skinned and chopped
25 ml (5 tsp) tomato purée
10 ml (2 tsp) light brown sugar
5 ml (1 tsp) sea salt and milled black pepper to taste
125 ml (4 fl oz) Marmite stock (see box on p. 60)

Put lentils into a saucepan with 750 ml (1¹/₄ pints) water and the salt, bring to the boil, cover and simmer for about 50 minutes until soft and liquid is absorbed.

Meanwhile, heat the sunflower oil in a large saucepan and sauté the onion, garlic, carrots and green pepper. When softening, add all the remaining ingredients, except the cooked lentils, stir to mix, then cover and simmer gently for 20-30 minutes, stirring occasionally to mash the tomatoes.

Stir in the cooked lentils and leave on low heat for 5-10 minutes, stirring once or twice. The mixture should be moist and juicy, so a low heat throughout is important. If a little thickening is necessary, you could stir in some toasted wheatgerm for extra nourishment, or do it the conventional way with a beurre manié. (See box on p. 53.) Serve as suggested.
*Serves 5–6.*

# SOYA BEAN CURRY

*This is one of the nicest bean dishes and an excellent introduction to soya beans for those not familiar with them. Served on brown rice, it also makes an incredibly low-cost meal. On the side, apart from the usual sambals such as chutney and sliced bananas, I like to serve a cabbage slaw tossed with plenty of coconut — it complements the curried beans perfectly. Also good is slivered avocado sprinkled with toasted sesame seeds. Allow sufficient time when making for the sauce to be cooled down and reheated for the full flavour to develop.*

60 ml (4 tbsp) sunflower oil
2 onions, chopped
10-15 ml (2-3 tsp) curry powder
2.5 ml (¹/₂ tsp) turmeric
5 ml (1 tsp) each ground cinnamon, cumin and fennel
1 knob root ginger, peeled and grated
2 cloves garlic, crushed
2 dessert apples, peeled and finely diced
2 large tomatoes, skinned and chopped
2 carrots, diced
2 sticks celery, sliced, plus some leaves
100 ml (7 tbsp) chopped parsley
5 ml (1 tsp) sea salt
20 ml (4 tsp) lemon juice
10 ml (2 tsp) honey
2 bay leaves
450 g (1 lb) cooked soya beans
75 g (2¹/₂ oz) seedless raisins
about 650 ml (22 fl oz) vegetable stock or water

Heat the sunflower oil in a large saucepan and fry the onions lightly. Add curry powder, all the spices, root ginger and garlic and stir briefly over low heat. Add all the remaining ingredients, mix well, bring to the boil, then cover and simmer very gently for about 25 minutes, stirring occasionally and adding a little extra water if necessary to keep mixture nice and moist. If preparing in advance, turn the curry into a suitable container, cool and chill.

Reheat gently before serving. Check the seasoning and remove the bay leaves.

Serve as suggested.
*Serves 6.*

*Spicy Two-Bean Stew (p. 68) and Ratatouille with Haricots (p. 68).*

# SPICY LENTIL CURRY

*A surprisingly delicious curry. Serve on rice with sambals and a tomato and onion salad.*

25 ml (5 tsp) sunflower oil
30 g (1 oz) butter
2 large onions, sliced
1 green pepper, seeded and diced
2 cloves garlic, crushed
2 sticks celery, thinly sliced
3 carrots, coarsely grated
10 ml (2 tsp) curry powder
5 ml (1 tsp) each ground cumin, turmeric and ground fennel
300 g (11 oz) brown lentils, picked over and rinsed
1 bay leaf
100 ml (7 tbsp) chopped parsley
5 ml (1 tsp) sea salt
10 ml (2 tsp) brown sugar
175 ml (6 fl oz) tomato purée
a few spoonfuls of soured cream
snipped chives and/or chopped cashew nuts for topping

Heat oil and butter and sauté onions, green pepper, garlic, celery and carrots. When softened, add spices and stir over low heat for a few minutes.

Add lentils, 750 ml (1¼ pints) water, bay leaf, parsley, salt, sugar and tomato purée. Mix well and spoon into a large baking dish. Bake, covered, at 180°C (350°F, gas 4) for about 1 hour, or until lentils are soft, stirring once or twice. Remove from oven and streak in a few spoonfuls of soured cream, sprinkle with chives and/or cashews and warm through for another 5 minutes before serving.
*Serves 6.*

---

### SAUCEPANS
·

Dishes like curries and other spicy mixtures are often best made in advance and left to stand for the flavours to develop before re-heating. As these dishes usually contain an acidic ingredient, like tomatoes, wine or chutney, they should not be left in the saucepan to cool, especially an aluminium or other metallic saucepan, which will react with acid. In any case, if you are still using aluminium cookware, perhaps it is time to invest in good quality, heavy stainless steel saucepans or baked enamelware.

---

### HARICOT BEANS
·

Soak overnight in plenty of cold water. Drain, rinse and place in saucepan. Cover with water and simmer until soft, adding salt after 30 minutes. An alternative method is to bring the beans to the boil in a generous quantity of water, and then leave to soak for 2 hours. Drain and rinse, cover with fresh water, and boil until soft.

---

# HARICOT BEAN AND PUMPKIN CASSEROLE

*This is a good choice for a simple but nourishing family meal. Serve with brown rice and creamed spinach spiced with nutmeg.*

250 g (9 oz) haricot beans
45 ml (3 tbsp) sunflower oil
1 large onion, chopped
2 cloves garlic, crushed
500 g (18 oz) peeled, firm orange pumpkin
2 bay leaves
2.5 ml (½ tsp) ground cinnamon
5 ml (1 tsp) each ground coriander and ginger
15 ml (1 tbsp) honey
7.5-10 ml (1½-2 tsp) sea salt
15 g (½ oz) chopped parsley
400 g (14 oz) canned tomatoes, drained and chopped, juice reserved

TOPPING
45 g (1½ oz) fine, fresh wholewheat breadcrumbs
60 g (2 oz) finely grated, strong Cheddar cheese
25 ml (5 tsp) toasted sesame seeds

Soak beans overnight. Drain and rinse.

Heat oil in a large saucepan and fry onion and garlic. Add beans and 500 ml (17 fl oz) water. Bring to the boil, reduce heat, cover and simmer for 20 minutes. Cut pumpkin into dice-sized cubes and add, together with bay leaves, spices, honey, salt, parsley and tomatoes. Cover and simmer for about 50 minutes or until beans are tender, stirring occasionally.

If vegetables have not cooked to a pulp at end of cooking time, mash gently with a wooden spoon to make a thick sauce, taking care not to break up the beans.

---

Check seasoning and, if necessary, add the reserved tomato juice to ensure a moist mixture. Remove the bay leaves and spoon the mixture into a 30 × 20-cm (12 × 8-in) baking dish. If preparing in advance, set the casserole aside at this stage.

Just before baking, mix all the ingredients for the topping and sprinkle over the casserole. Bake, uncovered, at 180°C (350°F, gas 4) for about 30 minutes, until hot and bubbling. Serve as suggested.
*Serves 6.*

---

# LENTILS AND AUBERGINES IN BARBECUE SAUCE

*A thick, savoury stew, which is delicious served on pasta or brown rice, topped with crumbled feta or grated Cheddar or Parmesan cheese. A lettuce and avocado salad tossed with French dressing is a good accompaniment, with crusty rolls an optional extra.*

200 g (7 oz) brown lentils, picked over and rinsed
45 ml (3 tbsp) sunflower oil
300 g (11 oz) young aubergines, cubed or 1 medium aubergine, cubed and dégorged
1 large onion, chopped
2 cloves garlic, crushed
1 small green or red pepper, seeded and diced
200 g (7 oz) baby marrows, scrubbed and sliced
250 ml (8 fl oz) tomato passata
15 ml (1 tbsp) honey
25 ml (5 tsp) soy sauce
100 ml (7 tbsp) chopped parsley
250 ml (8 fl oz) water
5 ml (1 tsp) dried basil

Boil lentils gently in 500 ml (17 fl oz) salted water for about 50 minutes until soft.

Meanwhile, heat the sunflower oil in a large pan and add the aubergines, onion, garlic, pepper and baby marrows. Toss over low heat for 5 minutes. Add the remaining ingredients, except the cooked lentils, cover and simmer gently for 30 minutes.

Add cooked lentils and, if necessary, another 125 ml (4 fl oz) water, or enough to make a good sauce. Simmer very gently for another 15 minutes.

Adjust seasoning — it may need a pinch of sea salt or a little sugar — and serve as suggested above.
*Serves 4.*

# LENTIL AND POTATO PIE

*Brown lentils are a good source of plant protein and if you like their distinctive, rather earthy flavour, you'll enjoy this pie, in which they're baked between layers of sliced potatoes and onions and topped with cheese. This simple dish is one of our favourite vegetarian meals, especially when accompanied with buttered cabbage and baked pumpkin.*

300 g (11 oz) brown lentils, picked over
and rinsed
750 g (1½ lb) potatoes, thinly sliced
2 large onions, thinly sliced
salt and milled black pepper to taste
750 ml (1¼ pints) hot stock or 10 ml
(2 tsp) Marmite in 750 ml (1¼ pints)
hot water
grated Cheddar cheese for topping
butter for topping
paprika for topping

Cover lentils with water and leave to soak for about 2 hours. Grease a deep 23-cm (9-in) pie dish and cover the base with half the potatoes and onions. Season lightly. Top with drained lentils, spreading evenly. Cover with remaining onions and potatoes, and season lightly again. Pour hot stock over the mixture, cover with greased foil, shiny side up (or with a lid) and bake at 180°C (350°F, gas 4) for 1 hour.

Remove cover and sprinkle thickly with cheese, dot with butter and dust with paprika. Bake, uncovered, for a further 20 minutes, by which time potatoes and lentils should be soft, liquid absorbed and cheese melted and bubbling.
*Serves 6–8.*

---

## SPLIT PEAS

They are usually reserved for soups, which is a pity. Green split peas are tasty, nutritious, and do not need pre-soaking. They will, in fact, cook to a mush in about 30 minutes. (Use 200 g (7 oz) rinsed peas to 750 ml (1¼ pints) water.) I even cook them in the oven, if it is already on. Use the same quantities as when boiling them, and cover the baking dish. When soft, they can be puréed and served instead of mashed potatoes. They are an economical and neglected pulse.

---

## NUTS AND SUNFLOWER SEEDS

Nuts are expensive but indispensable in any kitchen. I buy them in bulk and keep them in the freezer. Chopping in a food processor makes them go further. Use the grinding blade and be careful not to reduce them to powder. Toasting brings out the flavour. Spread the chopped nuts on baking trays and place them in a moderate oven until they are golden brown.

Sunflower seeds are much cheaper, rich in protein, vitamins and minerals, and can often be substituted for nuts. As they are often somewhat dusty, rinse them well in a colander first and then dry them out in a low oven, spread on baking trays. This is a nuisance as they take a while to dry, but dry they must or you cannot store them. For convenience, do a jumbo batch at a time and remember that their flavour is even better if they are slightly toasted.

---

# CASSEROLE OF LENTILS AND RICE WITH PIZZA TOPPING

*Serve with creamy mashed potatoes, cinnamon-baked pumpkin and a salad.*

200 g (7 oz) brown lentils, picked over
and rinsed
100 g (3½ oz) brown rice
25 ml (5 tsp) sunflower oil
15 g (½ oz) butter
2 medium onions, finely chopped
2 green or red peppers, seeded and diced
100 ml (7 tbsp) chopped parsley
45 g (1½ oz) fresh wholewheat
breadcrumbs
2 eggs
125 ml (4 fl oz) buttermilk
sea salt and milled black pepper to taste
3-4 firm tomatoes, thinly sliced
grated mozzarella or Cheddar cheese
grated Parmesan cheese
2.5 ml (½ tsp) dried oregano
1.25 ml (¼ tsp) dried basil
about 30 ml (2 tbsp) olive oil

Simmer lentils in 500 ml (17 fl oz) salted water for about 50 minutes. Cook rice in 300 ml (½ pint) salted water for about 45 minutes.

Heat oil and butter and sauté onions and peppers. Spoon lentils and rice into a large bowl and add cooked onions and peppers, parsley and breadcrumbs. Beat eggs with buttermilk and add to lentil and rice mixture together with seasoning. Mix well, without mashing, and spoon into a deep, buttered 23-cm (9-in) pie dish. Level top and cover with layers of tomatoes, plenty of grated mozzarella or Cheddar, and a sprinkling of Parmesan. Sprinkle herbs on top and drizzle with oil. Bake at 180°C (350°F, gas 4) for about 25 minutes, until cheese has melted.
*Serves 6.*

---

# POT BEANS

*This is a hot and savoury version of the popular fasoulia. Economical, easy to prepare and remarkably good served on brown rice with a green salad.*

500 g (18 oz) haricot beans
100 ml (7 tbsp) sunflower oil
2 large onions, chopped
5 ml (1 tsp) each dried thyme
and oregano
125 ml (4 fl oz) tomato purée
4 cloves garlic, crushed
2 bay leaves
15 ml (1 tbsp) honey
salt and milled black pepper to taste
vegetable stock or water
1 bunch spinach, shredded (optional)
15 g (½ oz) chopped parsley
soy sauce to taste
grated Cheddar cheese for
topping (optional)

Soak beans overnight, then drain and rinse.

Heat oil in a large saucepan and add onions. When softened, add beans and toss over medium heat for 5 minutes. Add herbs, tomato purée, garlic, bay leaves, honey and seasoning. Add enough stock or water to cover, then cover saucepan and simmer gently for 1½ hours, or until beans are soft and liquid is thick and reduced. Add spinach, if using, and parsley. Cover and simmer for another 30 minutes. To serve, add soy sauce to taste, then spoon over servings of rice and top with grated cheese.
*Serves 6–8.*

*Overleaf: Chickpea and Tomato Curry (p. 68) and Soya Bean Curry (p. 62), served with various side dishes.*

# RATATOUILLE WITH HARICOTS

*Here, traditional ratatouille — the delicious vegetable concoction from France — becomes an equally good vegetarian meal-in-a-dish with the addition of beans. Serve on brown rice, sprinkled with grated cheese.*

25 ml (5 tsp) each sunflower and
olive oil
2 large onions, chopped
2 cloves garlic, crushed
1 green pepper, seeded and diced
500 g (18 oz) aubergines, cubed
and dégorged
500 g (18 oz) baby marrows, pared
and sliced
5 ml (1 tsp) sea salt and milled black
pepper to taste
2 bay leaves
5 ml (1 tsp) dried oregano
5 ml (1 tsp) light brown sugar
500 g (18 oz) juicy tomatoes, skinned
and chopped
450 g (1 lb) cooked haricot or soya beans
chopped parsley for garnish

Heat oils in a large saucepan and add onions, garlic and green pepper. Cook very gently, without browning, for 10 minutes, shaking pan occasionally. When softened, add aubergines and marrows, seasoning, bay leaves, oregano and sugar. Mix well, then cover and leave to simmer slowly for about 20 minutes until not quite tender. Add tomatoes and beans. Mix well, then cover and simmer for another 20 minutes, or until everything is soft and juicy, adding just a little water if necessary. Never boil ratatouille to a mush — the vegetables should be identifiable. Remove bay leaves, check seasoning and sprinkle with parsley.
*Serves 6.*

# SPICY TWO-BEAN STEW

*This dish was created one evening when I unexpectedly had to feed some hungry vegetarians with little on hand but a few cups of left-over cooked beans. It has become a great favourite. It's easy, economical, delicious and very nourishing — and if you cook beans in bulk and freeze them, you can make it at almost a moment's notice. Serve on brown rice with bowls of coconut and chutney. A green salad should also accompany the meal.*

100 ml (3½ fl oz) sunflower oil
3 large onions, chopped
3 cloves garlic, crushed
10 ml (2 tsp) each turmeric, ground
cinnamon and curry powder
5 ml (1 tsp) ground cumin
450 g (1 lb) cooked soya beans
450 g (1 lb) cooked haricot beans
750 ml (1¼ pints) vegetable stock
or water
45 ml (3 tbsp) tomato purée
2 bay leaves
10 ml (2 tsp) each sea salt and light
brown sugar
175 g (6 oz) seedless raisins
45 ml (3 tbsp) chutney
parsley or chopped coriander leaves
for garnish (optional)

Heat oil in a large pan and soften onions and garlic. Add all the spices and allow to sizzle for a few minutes. Add remaining ingredients, except parsley or coriander, bring to the boil, then cover and simmer on lowest heat for about 45 minutes, stirring occasionally. By end of cooking period the sauce should be reduced, thick and flavoursome. Check seasoning and remove bay leaves. Sprinkle with parsley or coriander, if liked.
*Serves 6–8.*

# CHICKPEA AND TOMATO CURRY

*A mild, creamy curry, using basic ingredients; easy to prepare, and sure to become a favourite way of serving this protein-rich pulse.*

30 ml (2 tbsp) sunflower oil
1 large onion, finely chopped
2 cloves garlic, crushed
1 green pepper, seeded and diced
10 ml (2 tsp) curry powder
5 ml (1 tsp) each ground cinnamon
and coriander
2.5 ml (½ tsp) each turmeric and
ground cumin
500 g (18 oz) juicy tomatoes, skinned
and chopped
375 ml (12 fl oz) vegetable stock or water
15 ml (1 tbsp) tomato purée
5 ml (1 tsp) sea salt
2 bay leaves
10 ml (2 tsp) light brown sugar
550 g (19 oz) cooked chickpeas
100 ml (7 tbsp) chopped parsley
60 ml (4 tbsp) desiccated coconut
60 ml (4 tbsp) soured cream

Heat oil, add onion, garlic and green pepper and allow to soften. Add all the spices and stir for a minute or two to release the flavours. Add remaining ingredients, except coconut and soured cream. Bring to the boil, then cover and simmer gently for about 25 minutes, stirring occasionally.

If time allows, transfer to suitable container and cool before reheating. The dish may also be refrigerated overnight. Reheat over low heat, adding extra liquid as necessary for the sauce. Check seasoning, stir in coconut and when thoroughly heated, swirl in cream.
*Serves 4–6.*

---

## SOYA BEANS
·

Like 'em or not, soya beans — possibly the world's oldest food crop — are a highly concentrated source of vegetable protein. Rich in oil, yet low in carbohydrates, they also contain lecithin and plenty of fibre, as well as calcium and iron. Soya protein contains all eight amino acids essential for human needs.

Apart from oil and flour, the beans are also used to make TVP, see box on p. 69.

Soak overnight in plenty of cold water. Drain and tip into a large bowl. Add plenty of fresh water and then rub beans between palms of hands to remove skins (unlike chickpeas, from which skins are removed after cooking). As skins float to the top, pour off water. Repeat this process several times. If only some of the skins come off, don't worry as the rest will rise

to the top when the water starts to boil rapidly, so just skim them off with the froth a few times. Rubbing off the skins is seldom specified, but I always do, as they don't look nice floating on top of a dish, and must surely be indigestible.

To cook, simmer soya beans in water for about 2½ hours, adding salt towards the end of cooking period.

# VEGETARIAN BOBOTIE

*This recipe is a good one to start experimenting with TVP, an economical and healthy source of protein. Serve with buttered rice, cinnamon-baked pumpkin, a green vegetable and extra chutney.*

150 g (5 oz) soya mince
10 ml (2 tsp) Marmite, mixed with
750 ml (1¼ pints) boiling water
1 fairly thick slice crustless
wholewheat bread
375 ml (12 fl oz) milk
45 ml (3 tbsp) sunflower oil
2 large onions, chopped
2 cloves garlic, crushed
25 ml (5 tsp) curry powder
7.5 ml (1½ tsp) sea salt
25 ml (5 tsp) chutney
15 ml (1 tbsp) smooth apricot jam
15 ml (1 tbsp) Worcestershire sauce
5 ml (1 tsp) turmeric
15 ml (1 tbsp) brown vinegar
75 g (2½ oz) seedless raisins
100 ml (7 tbsp) chopped, toasted
almonds
3 eggs
a big pinch each of salt and turmeric
100 ml (7 tbsp) desiccated coconut
bay leaves

Place soya mince in a bowl, pour Marmite stock over it and leave to hydrate for 15 minutes.

Soak the wholewheat bread in the milk.

Heat the sunflower oil and lightly fry the onions and garlic. Add the curry powder and sizzle for a minute or two. Add the sea salt, chutney, jam, Worcestershire sauce, turmeric and vinegar and mix well.

Squeeze the soaked bread (reserve the milk) and add it to the pan together with the soya mince, which will be swollen, with almost all the liquid absorbed.

Add the raisins, almonds and 1 beaten egg and mix all the ingredients together.

Spoon the curry mixture into an oiled baking dish, no larger than 30 × 20 cm (12 × 8 in), spreading it evenly.

Beat the remaining 2 eggs with the reserved milk — you should not have less than 300 ml (½ pint). Add a big pinch each of salt and turmeric, and the coconut. Pour evenly over the curry mixture, and top with a few bay leaves.

Stand the baking dish in a large roasting tin of water and bake at 180°C (350°F, gas 4) for 1 hour. Serve as suggested.
*Makes 6 large servings.*

---

## TVP

Some people may query the sense in using this meat substitute (which does not taste anything like the real thing) in a vegetarian diet. But TVP (textured vegetable protein) or TSP (textured soya protein) is such a powerful, protein-rich food, and so economical, that it is worth experimenting with this soya bean product in home-made dishes. You're probably eating TVP anyway, without knowing it, tucked into all sorts of manufactured foods, such as an extender in meat products, to ensure freshness in biscuits, and so on. It is available as granules and chunks, which need to be re-hydrated before use.

---

# VEGETARIAN BOLOGNAISE

*Vegetarians who use soya mince to add protein to their diets should find this recipe useful. Although it looks just like the traditional meaty sauce so often served with pasta, the flavour and texture are totally different, and although TVP might not be to everybody's taste, it does make a singularly nourishing and economical meal.*

150 g (5 oz) soya mince
10 ml (2 tsp) Marmite, mixed with
750 ml (1¼ pints) hot water
25 ml (5 tsp) sunflower oil
30 g (1 oz) butter
2 large onions, chopped
2 cloves garlic, crushed
1 green pepper, seeded and diced
5 ml (1 tsp) dried oregano
2.5 ml (½ tsp) dried thyme
400 g (14 oz) canned tomatoes, chopped,
plus the juice
125 ml (4 fl oz) tomato passata
5 ml (1 tsp) sea salt
10 ml (2 tsp) light brown sugar
100 ml (7 tbsp) red wine
100 ml (7 tbsp) chopped parsley
45 ml (3 tbsp) grated Parmesan cheese

Place soya mince in a bowl, pour over Marmite stock and stand for 15 minutes. Heat oil and butter in a large frying pan and lightly fry onions, garlic and green pepper. Add herbs and toss until hot and aromatic.

Add mince and remaining ingredients, except cheese. Bring to the boil, then cover and simmer very gently for 45 minutes, stirring occasionally. When done, the sauce should be thick and juicy.

Stir in the Parmesan, heat through and serve on pasta, brown rice or with mashed potatoes. If serving on pasta, serve extra Parmesan separately.
*Makes 6 large servings.*

---

# TOFU WITH MUSHROOMS, ONIONS AND CHEESE

*Tofu is a soya bean curd, widely used in Japanese cooking. It is bland in flavour, high in protein and low in fat and may be found in wholefood shops. Once purchased, you should take it home, cover it with water and chill, as it goes off very quickly. It may be served in salads, soups and sauces, or in a casserole as in this recipe. As it is served here in the dish in which it was cooked, use a presentable frying pan or a serving dish which can be placed on top of the stove. Serve on brown rice, or rice mixed with cooked brown lentils in equal quantities and tossed with a little finely chopped parsley and a nut of butter, with an accompaniment of a fresh green salad or vegetables.*

25 ml (5 tsp) sunflower oil
15 g (½ oz) butter
2 large onions, thinly sliced
30-45 ml (2-3 tbsp) soy sauce
250 g (9 oz) brown mushrooms, wiped
and sliced
1 green pepper, seeded and diced
250 g (9 oz) tofu
45 ml (3 tbsp) toasted sesame seeds
25 ml (5 tsp) sherry
grated Cheddar cheese

Place oil, butter, onions, 30 ml (2 tbsp) soy sauce, mushrooms and green pepper in saucepan. Cover and cook over low heat for about 10 minutes until softened.

Meanwhile, pat tofu dry (using paper towels), cut into cubes and roll the cubes in sesame seeds.

Add the sherry and extra soy sauce to taste to the mixture in the pan. Top with the tofu cubes, cover and simmer gently for 10 minutes. Sprinkle generously with the grated Cheddar cheese, turn off heat and leave for 5 minutes before serving.

Serve as suggested.
*Makes 4 large servings.*

# VEGETABLES

## VEGETABLE PAELLA

45 ml (3 tbsp) each sunflower
and olive oil
2 large leeks, sliced
1 onion, chopped
3 cloves garlic, crushed
1 green pepper, seeded and diced
300 g (11 oz) brown rice
250 g (9 oz) mushrooms, wiped
and sliced
250 g (9 oz) aubergines, dégorged
and diced
5 ml (1 tsp) each turmeric, dried oregano
and dried basil
400 g (14 oz) tomatoes, skinned
and chopped
250 g (9 oz) chopped green beans or
325 g (12 oz) peas
100 ml (7 tbsp) chopped parsley
sea salt and milled black pepper to taste
a pinch of sugar
500 ml (17 fl oz) vegetable or
Marmite stock
125 ml (4 fl oz) white wine
250 g (9 oz) feta cheese, diced

Using a large saucepan, heat oils and add
leeks, onion, garlic and green pepper. When
softened, add rice and toss until coated
with oil. Reduce heat and add mushrooms,
aubergines, turmeric and herbs. Toss for a
minute or two, then add tomatoes (or can of
tomatoes, plus the juice), beans or peas,
parsley, seasoning, sugar, stock and wine.
Mix well, then turn into a 30 × 25-cm (12 ×
10-in) baking dish. Cover and bake at 180°C
(350°F, gas 4) for 35 minutes. Stir lightly
with a fork, then continue baking for
another 20-25 minutes until vegetables are
cooked and the liquid absorbed. The mixture should be moist but not at all watery.
Turn off oven and cover top with diced feta
and return to oven for 5-10 minutes to heat
through.
*Serves 6.*

*Vegetable Stir-Fry with Noodles and
Chinese Sauce (p. 80).*

# SPICY FRUIT AND VEGETABLE CURRY

*One can use almost any combination of ingredients; this is a good, basic version. Although the list of ingredients is long, they are mostly familiar items. Serve on brown or Basmati rice with extra chutney and coconut on the side and a tomato and onion salad.*

100 ml (7 tbsp) sunflower oil
2 large onions, finely chopped
3 cloves garlic, crushed
1 knob root ginger, peeled and grated
15-20 ml (3-4 tsp) curry powder
5 ml (1 tsp) each ground cinnamon,
turmeric, coriander and
green cardamom
2.5 ml (½ tsp) ground cumin
4 carrots, finely diced
2 dessert apples, peeled and diced
2 large sticks celery, chopped,
plus a few leaves
325 g (12 oz) shredded cabbage
½ small head cauliflower florets
600 ml (1 pint) vegetable stock
or water
10 ml (2 tsp) sea salt
45 g (1½ oz) desiccated coconut
45 ml (3 tbsp) chutney
90 g (3 oz) seedless raisins
25 ml (5 tsp) fresh lemon juice
3 bay leaves
10 ml (2 tsp) honey
2 bananas, thinly sliced
60 g (2 oz) toasted almond strips
soured cream

Heat the sunflower oil in a very large, deep saucepan and gently fry the onion, garlic and ginger. Add all the spices and toss until sizzling. Add the carrots, apples, table celery, shredded cabbage and cauliflower florets. Toss over low heat until vegetables are coated with spices, then add the stock or water, sea salt, coconut, chutney, raisins, lemon juice, bay leaves and honey. Bring to the boil, mix well, then cover and simmer over low heat for about 20 minutes, stirring occasionally without breaking up the cauliflower and adding a little more stock or water if necessary.

If time allows, cool the curry, transfer to a suitable non-metallic container, and refrigerate overnight for flavours to blend.

To serve, remove the bay leaves and reheat the curry gently. Mix in the bananas, almond strips and enough soured cream to make a good sauce and bring to full heat, without boiling. Serve as suggested.
*Serves 8.*

# PHYLLO PARCELS WITH BEAN SPROUTS, FETA AND ALMONDS

*This vegetable mixture makes a delicious filling. Serve with Tzatziki (p. 76) and a creamy cabbage salad. Tissue-thin, feathery phyllo pastry requires special treatment (see box).*

500 g (18 oz) frozen phyllo pastry,
thawed in refrigerator for 24 hours
oil or melted butter

FILLING
125 g (4 oz) mung bean sprouts
200 g (7 oz) feta cheese, rinsed and diced
60 g (2 oz) chopped toasted almonds
2 egg yolks
25 ml (5 tsp) soy sauce
2 sticks celery, finely chopped
6 spring onions, chopped
4 small baby marrows, pared and
coarsely grated
a pinch of sugar

Combine ingredients for filling. Remove 3 sheets of phyllo — they should measure about 43 × 37 cm (17 × 15 in). Brush each sheet with oil, garlic oil or melted butter (or, if cutting down on fat, brush only the top sheet; the results will be just as good), and place the sheets one on top of the other. Place a mound of filling in the centre and then draw up the corners to form a parcel, twisting the top to seal. Brush with oil or butter and sprinkle lightly with water. Make five more parcels in the same way, place on two large, oiled baking sheets and bake at 200°C (400°F, gas 6) for 20 minutes until golden brown.
*Makes 6 parcels.*

---

## USING PHYLLO PASTRY

·

The day before using, transfer phyllo to refrigerator. Unwrap and lay out on a dry tea-towel. Cover with another tea-towel, then with a damp one, and leave for 10 minutes, always keeping the sheets you are not working with covered in this way. They quickly become brittle when exposed to air.

Brush each sheet (or only the top sheet) lightly with melted butter (for sweet or savoury dishes) or oil (for savoury dishes) before using.

---

## MUSHROOM CROSTINI

·

This makes a marvellous, one-mouthful snack to serve with drinks. Not only are the crisp bread rounds (piled with an aromatic topping) perfect finger food as they do not drip, but the topping can be made and chilled the day before, the bread cut and crisped hours in advance, and the whole lot can be assembled, refrigerated until needed and baked just before serving.

**12-16 slices slightly stale**
**white or plain brown bread**
**15 g (½ oz) butter and**
**45 ml (3 tbsp) oil, melted**
**together**
**45 g (1½ oz) butter**
**250 g (9 oz) white or brown**
**mushrooms, wiped and**
**very finely chopped**
**45 ml (3 tbsp) white flour**
**250 ml (8 fl oz) milk**
**6 spring onions, finely**
**chopped**
**1.25 ml (¼ tsp) dried**
**oregano, crushed**
**sea salt and milled black**
**pepper to taste**
**8 olives, stoned and**
**slivered**
**grated Parmesan cheese**

Slice crusts off bread and stamp out rounds using a 5-cm (2-in) biscuit cutter. Place rounds on a baking tray and brush both sides with the melted butter and oil. Bake at 180°C (350°F, gas 4) for 10-12 minutes, until golden brown and crisp, turning once. Cool.

Melt the 45 g (1½ oz) butter in a small pan, add mushrooms and toss over low heat until soft and all liquid has evaporated. Sprinkle in flour, slowly add milk, bring to the boil, and stir until very thick. Remove from heat and add onions, oregano and seasoning to taste. If working ahead, cool, cover and refrigerate until needed.

To bake, spread the mushroom mixture thickly on each bread round, top with the slivered olives, if using, and sprinkle with the grated Parmesan. Bake at 200°C (400°F, gas 6) for 12-15 minutes until piping hot. Serve at once.
*Makes about 36, depending on size.*

# VEGETABLE COTTAGE PIE (1)

*This is a large simple pie, but nourishing and inexpensive. Apart from the topping, it may be assembled in advance.*

150 g (5 oz) brown rice
200 g (7 oz) brown lentils, picked over and rinsed
25 ml (5 tsp) sunflower oil
1 large onion, chopped
2 cloves garlic, crushed
3 carrots, finely diced
5 ml (1 tsp) mixed dried herbs
300 g (11 oz) juicy tomatoes, skinned and chopped
175 g (6 oz) shredded cabbage
15 g (½ oz) chopped parsley
3 eggs, beaten
250 ml (8 fl oz) buttermilk
125 g (4 oz) grated Cheddar cheese
25 ml (5 tsp) soy sauce
4 large potatoes, scrubbed
a little hot milk
a few nuts of butter

Cook the rice in 450 ml (¾ pint) salted water until done. Cook the lentils in 500 ml (17 fl oz) salted water until soft and water is absorbed. Meanwhile, heat oil in small frying pan. Sauté onions and garlic and when softened add the carrots, herbs and tomatoes. Cover and simmer until the tomatoes are pulpy – for about 10 minutes.

Tip cooked rice and lentils into a large bowl. Add cabbage, parsley, eggs, buttermilk, 60 g (2 oz) cheese and the soy sauce. Do not add salt, as the soy sauce should salt it sufficiently. Add tomato mixture and mix gently but thoroughly. Spoon into a lightly oiled 30 × 20-cm (12 × 8-in) baking dish, spreading evenly. Heat oven to 160°C (325°F, gas 3) and bake, covered, for 35 minutes.

Meanwhile, boil potatoes until soft. Mash with milk and butter, then swirl over pie. Sprinkle with rest of cheese, and return to oven, uncovered, for about 20 minutes until hot and cheese has melted.
*Makes 6 large servings.*

# VEGETABLE COTTAGE PIE (2)

*As vegetables and rice do not constitute a complete meal, it is a good idea to add lentils as a complementary protein. Also, when mixed with rice, their somewhat dominant flavour is mellowed. Served with baked pumpkin and peas or a green salad, this dish makes a satisfying, simple meal. You can use left-over rice or lentils.*

30 g (1 oz) butter
25 ml (5 tsp) sunflower oil
1 large onion, chopped
2 cloves garlic, crushed
4 medium carrots, julienned
2 sticks celery, plus some leaves, chopped
1 green or red pepper, seeded and diced
250 g (9 oz) brown or white mushrooms, wiped and sliced
400 g (14 oz) canned tomatoes, chopped, plus the juice
100 ml (7 tbsp) chopped parsley
150 g (5 oz) coarsely shredded spinach
2.5 ml (½ tsp) sea salt and generous pinch of sugar
250 g (9 oz) cooked brown rice
175 g (6 oz) cooked brown or green lentils
25 ml (5 tsp) soy sauce
30 ml (2 tbsp) chopped fresh mixed herbs (e.g. thyme, marjoram and sage)
potatoes mashed with a little milk and butter
125 g (4 oz) grated Cheddar cheese

Use a large, deep saucepan in which to heat butter and oil. Sauté onion and garlic. Add carrots, celery, pepper and mushrooms and toss until softening. Add tomatoes, parsley, spinach, salt and sugar, mix well, then cover and simmer until just cooked — for about 6 minutes. The mixture should be moist. Lightly fork in rice, lentils, soy sauce and herbs and when combined, spoon into an oiled 30 × 20-cm (12 × 8-in) baking dish. Cover with mashed potatoes, sprinkle with cheese, and bake at 160°C (325°F, gas 3) for 40 minutes.
*Serves 8.*

# CHEESE-TOPPED VEGETABLE BAKE

*The sort of wholesome dish you'd expect to find at an unpretentious vegetarian restaurant. Rice and lentils add substance. Serve with a salad or vegetables, like new potatoes, creamed spinach, stuffed aubergines or stir-fried baby marrows.*

60 ml (4 tbsp) sunflower oil
2 large onions, chopped
2 cloves garlic, crushed
2 large sticks celery, plus some leaves, chopped
250 g (9 oz) brown mushrooms, wiped and sliced
250 g (9 oz) coarsely grated raw butternut squash
150 g (5 oz) brown rice
150 g (5 oz) brown lentils, picked over and rinsed
5 ml (1 tsp) dried oregano
2.5 ml (½ tsp) dried thyme
800 ml (27 fl oz) hot Marmite stock
5 ml (1 tsp) sea salt
100 ml (7 tbsp) chopped parsley
45 ml (3 tbsp) soy sauce
60 g (2 oz) bean sprouts

TOPPING
125 ml (4 fl oz) buttermilk
125 ml (4 fl oz) soured cream
2 eggs, separated
2.5 ml (½ tsp) sea salt and a pinch of sugar
5 ml (1 tsp) prepared mustard
125 g (4 oz) finely grated Cheddar cheese
paprika

Heat oil and sauté onion and garlic. Add celery, mushrooms and butternut. When softening and smelling good, but not shrunken, turn off heat and mix in remaining ingredients, except bean sprouts. Turn into an oiled baking dish — a deep, 25-cm (10-in) pie dish is ideal — and spread evenly. Cover and bake at 160°C (325°F, gas 3) for 1 hour. Remove and fork in the bean sprouts. For topping, whisk together buttermilk, cream, egg yolks, salt, pinch sugar, mustard and half the cheese. Stiffly whisk egg whites and fold in. Pour over baked mixture, sprinkle with remaining cheese and paprika, and bake uncovered for 20-25 minutes or until set.
*Serves 8.*

*Overleaf: Greek Green Bean and Aubergine Casserole (p. 88), Baked Souffléd Potatoes (p. 76) and Vegetable Cottage Pie (1) (this page).*

---

### PESTICIDES AND VEGETABLES

•

To pare or not to pare vegetables like baby marrows and cucumbers is a matter of choice. It's a pity to do so, but I do, because of the pesticides used on our vegetables. Tomatoes should also be well washed if you are using them with their skins.

# SPINACH AND FETA PIE WITH TZATZIKI

*My version of the popular Greek pie with phyllo, using bought puff pastry to simplify preparation. It's a super recipe which may be prepared and chilled until about 40 minutes before dinner, then baked and served piping hot, golden brown and plump with filling. The one proviso is that you must use fresh spinach. You will also need a very large saucepan. The recipe for tzatziki is a short-cut method, side-stepping the need to drain the yoghurt overnight.*

## TZATZIKI

½ small cucumber
250 ml (8 fl oz) thick Bulgarian yoghurt
1 small clove garlic, crushed
a pinch of sea salt
10 ml (2 tsp) finely chopped fresh mint
10 ml (2 tsp) olive oil
a pinch of sugar

Pare and grate cucumber coarsely and leave, weighted, to drain in a colander for about 20 minutes. Squeeze dry between paper towels, then fold all ingredients together until well mixed. Cover and chill for several hours.
*Makes about 250 ml (8 fl oz).*

## PIE

2 large bunches fresh spinach
25 ml (5 tsp) each sunflower
and olive oil
2 large onions, finely chopped
2 cloves garlic, crushed
5 ml (1 tsp) dried dill
2.5 ml (½ tsp) dried oregano
3 eggs, beaten
250 g (9 oz) feta cheese, rinsed
and crumbled
2.5 ml (½ tsp) sea salt and milled black
pepper to taste
30-45 ml (2-3 tbsp) grated
Parmesan cheese
400 g (14 oz) frozen puff pastry, thawed
in refrigerator
milk or lightly beaten egg for glazing

Trim stalks from spinach – weight should then be about 500 g (18 oz). Wash and shake dry.

Heat oils in a very large saucepan and soften onions and garlic. Add herbs and spinach leaves, cover and cook until soft, tossing now and then to mix. If spinach draws moisture, cook over high heat for 1-2 minutes, then drain very well in a colander. When cool, chop finely, and tip into a large bowl. Mix in eggs, feta, seasoning and Parmesan.

Dampen a 25 × 20-cm (10 × 8-in) baking tin. Line base of tin with half of pastry — should just cover the bottom. Spread spinach mixture evenly over top, then cover with rest of pastry. With dampened fingers, pinch all round edges to seal, and mark into six large squares.* If preparing in advance, chill at this stage.

Brush with milk or egg-wash and bake at 220°C (425°F, gas 7) for about 40 minutes or until pastry is golden brown and puffed. Slice through squares and serve.
*Serves 6.*

* Or make crescent-shaped pies, using double the given quantity of puff pastry, cut into twelve 15-cm (6-in) circles. Divide filling between them, spooning down one side, fold over, damp edges and seal with fork. Brush with milk or egg-wash and bake on dampened sheet for 30 minutes.

# STUFFED BAKED POTATOES

*This simple stuffing makes a change from plain baked potatoes. Serve with a salad for an inexpensive, light meal or team up with a bean casserole for heartier appetites.*

4 large baking potatoes
30 g (1 oz) butter, melted
about 150 ml (¼ pint) hot milk
125 g (4 oz) grated Cheddar cheese
sea salt and milled black pepper to taste
2.5 ml (½ tsp) prepared mustard
30 ml (2 tbsp) chopped parsley
paprika

Scrub potatoes, prick, rub skins with oil and bake at 200°C (400°F, gas 6) for about 1 hour until soft. Slice off the tops. Scoop flesh into a bowl, leaving a firm shell. Mash with the melted butter and milk, then add remaining ingredients, except paprika. Pile into shells, brush lightly with milk and dust with paprika, or top with a little more cheese and a small knob of butter. Reheat at 180°C (350°F, gas 4).
*Serves 4.*

> To avoid having to stand and toss a stir-fry all the time, I add a dash of water, and, with the pan three-quarters covered, let the steam do the cooking. Just toss now and then.

# BAKED SOUFFLÉD POTATOES

*Big potatoes, first baked and then stuffed with a mixture of cheese, spinach and eggs, then baked again until puffy and golden brown — these make a marvellous change from the usual baked spud and soured cream. I always serve them with a rather special bean salad, which is quite the nicest accompaniment: sliced green beans, garlic onions, and diced red pepper, stir-fried in sesame oil with a dash of sherry, soy sauce and lemon juice added, and then left to marinate until cold. Just before serving, I add a handful of chopped walnuts.*

8 large baking potatoes, scrubbed,
pricked and brushed with oil
12 large leaves spinach or Swiss chard
45 g (1½ oz) soft butter
125 g (4 oz) finely grated Cheddar
cheese
10 ml (2 tsp) prepared mild mustard
4 eggs, separated
6 spring onions, chopped
5 ml (1 tsp) sea salt and milled black
pepper to taste
a big pinch of grated nutmeg
about 100 ml (7 tbsp) milk

TOPPING
60 ml (4 tbsp) finely grated
Cheddar cheese
slivers of butter (optional)

Bake the potatoes at 200°C (400°F, gas 6) for an hour and 15 minutes or until cooked.

Meanwhile, blanch the spinach leaves in boiling water for a few minutes, then drain and chop finely.

As soon as potatoes are cool enough to handle, cut a slice about 1 cm (½ in) thick across the tops and scoop out the insides into a large bowl, leaving just enough of a 'lining' to keep the shells firm and standing upright. Arrange them close together in a lightly oiled baking dish.

Mash the scooped-out potato well with the butter, cheese, mustard, egg yolks, onions, seasoning, nutmeg, spinach and just enough milk to make a softish but *not* sloppy mixture. Stiffly whisk the egg whites and fold in.

Mound the filling into the shells. Top each potato with the extra cheese and place a sliver of butter, if using, on each. Return to oven for 20-25 minutes.

Serve, as suggested, with a bean salad (see notes above).
*Serves 8, with the salad.*

# VEGETABLE CURRY WITH COCONUT MILK AND RAITA

*A simple but delicious curry with a subtle mix of flavours which is particularly good served on top of spiced mixed rice and vegetables. The Raita should be made in advance and refrigerated, preferably overnight. Prepare the Coconut Milk before starting to make the Curry.*

## RAITA

250 ml (8 fl oz) Bulgarian yoghurt*
4-cm (1½-in) piece cucumber, pared, seeded and diced
2 spring onions, chopped
25 ml (5 tsp) finely chopped parsley
a pinch of sea salt
25 ml (5 tsp) chopped fresh mint
1.25 ml (¼ tsp) ground cumin

Fold all the ingredients together and then chill, covered.

* For a slightly thicker consistency, the yoghurt may first be drained in a muslin-lined sieve, but this is not essential.

## COCONUT MILK

90 g (3 oz) desiccated coconut
500 ml (17 fl oz) boiling water

Pour water over coconut and stand until cold. Strain, pressing as much liquid through sieve as possible. Reserve coconut.

## CURRY

45 ml (3 tbsp) sunflower oil
15 ml (1 tbsp) brown mustard seeds
2 large onions, chopped
2 cloves garlic, crushed
1 red pepper, seeded and diced
20-25 ml (4-5 tsp) curry powder
5 ml (1 tsp) each ground cumin and turmeric
6 white cardamom pods
2 star anise
400 g (14 oz) aubergines, cubed and dégorged
6 medium carrots, julienned
500 g (18 oz) cauliflower florets
400 g (14 oz) ripe tomatoes, skinned and chopped
2 sticks cinnamon
2 bay leaves
5 ml (1 tsp) each sea salt and light brown sugar
250 ml (8 fl oz) vegetable stock or water

Heat oil in a large pan, add mustard seeds and fry over medium heat until sizzling. If heat is too high, they'll pop right out of the pan. Add onions, garlic and red pepper. When softening, add curry powder and spices and toss for 1-2 minutes. Mix in aubergines, carrots and cauliflower and when coated with spices, add rest of ingredients and Coconut Milk. Bring to boil, then cover and simmer on lowest heat, stirring occasionally, for 30 minutes or until mixture has thickened and vegetables are cooked. Remove cinnamon, anise and bay leaves and, if possible, transfer to suitable container and cool for flavours to develop.

To reheat, add a little vegetable stock or water, if necessary, and check seasoning. It will probably need a little salt. Stir in reserved coconut. It will add flavour and thicken the juices. Serve on a mixture of cooked rice and lentils, handing the Raita and a bowl of chutney separately.
*Serves 8.*

# BAKED POTATOES WITH CHUNKY TOPPING

*The humble baked spud rises to new heights when served with this tasty topping — a mixture of lightly fried vegetables, cottage cheese and soured cream. Chunky cottage, rather than smooth soft cheese is always nicest with baked potatoes, but those little lumps do nothing for the appearance of the dish. So, use a bit of camouflage: before serving, spoon the mixture into a pretty pottery bowl and cover entirely with the sesame seeds, parsley or chives. Serve with steamed vegetables or a crisp salad.*

6 large baking potatoes, scrubbed, pricked and brushed with oil

### TOPPING
45 ml (3 tbsp) sunflower oil
1 onion, finely chopped
1-2 cloves garlic, crushed
1 red pepper, seeded and finely diced
250 g (9 oz) brown mushrooms, wiped and finely chopped
2 sprigs fresh rosemary
45 ml (3 tbsp) sweet sherry
25 ml (5 tsp) soy sauce
250 g (9 oz) cottage cheese
a little sea salt and milled black pepper to taste
125 ml (4 fl oz) soured cream
several pats of garlic or herbed butter
toasted sesame seeds or chopped chives or parsley for garnish

Bake potatoes at 200°C (400°F, gas 6) until cooked.

Meanwhile, heat the sunflower oil in a large pan and lightly fry the onion, garlic and red pepper. Add the mushrooms and rosemary and stir-fry over medium heat until softened and browned. Add sherry and soy sauce and continue cooking until mixture is shiny and moist, but all moisture must have evaporated. Spoon mixture into a bowl, removed rosemary and cool. Mix in cheese and soured cream, check seasoning and set aside until potatoes are cooked.

Serve one potato per person; cut a cross in the potato, squeeze to open, top with a pat of the garlic or herbed butter, then spoon topping over. Sprinkle with garnish.
*Serves 6.*

*Overleaf: Spicy Fruit and Vegetable Curry (p. 72), and Vegetable Paella (p. 71), served with chopped tomato and onion.*

# VEGETABLE STIR-FRY WITH NOODLES AND CHINESE SAUCE

*An attractive and succulent stir-fry, combining green beans, baby marrows and cucumber in a tasty brown sauce, with the subtle flavours of ginger and sesame adding an Oriental touch.*

30 ml (2 tbsp) sunflower oil
15 ml (1 tbsp) dark sesame oil
2 large leeks, sliced
1 small onion, chopped
1 red pepper, seeded and diced
2-3 cloves garlic, crushed
300 g (11 oz) young green beans, trimmed and sliced
300 g (11 oz) baby marrows, pared and julienned
1/2 cucumber, pared and julienned
225 g (8 oz) rice-shaped noodles
30 ml (2 tbsp) toasted sesame seeds
toasted, slivered almonds for garnish

SAUCE
375 ml (13 fl oz) vegetable stock or water
1 small knob fresh root ginger, peeled and grated
15 ml (1 tbsp) sherry
25 ml (5 tsp) cornflour
5 ml (1 tsp) honey
20 ml (4 tsp) soy sauce
15 ml (1 tbsp) lemon juice

Heat sunflower and sesame oils in a large pan. Add leeks, onion, red pepper and garlic and allow to soften. Add beans, marrows, cucumber and 45 ml (3 tbsp) water and cook until tender-crisp. As raw beans are not nice, the water is added to encourage steaming, and if the pan is half-covered and on medium heat, the vegetables should cook through while remaining succulent. Toss occasionally, using a wooden spoon. When ready for the sauce, the vegetable mixture will have reduced considerably.

Meanwhile, cook noodles quickly in plenty of rapidly boiling salted water, drain well, then toss with a dash of oil and the sesame seeds. Take care that the noodles don't become stodgy and stick together.

For the sauce, whisk together all the ingredients. Add it to the vegetable stir-fry mixture and bring to the boil, stirring. Check seasoning and serve at once, ladling the lovely thick vegetable mixture over each serving of noodles. Top generously with the slivered almonds.
*Makes 4 large servings*

---

### CELERY
•

Wash well, strip off the outer 'strings' from the thick ribs, and then slice thinly on the diagonal. Use very sparingly in salads, or more liberally in stir-fries.

---

# STIR-FRY WITH CAULIFLOWER, GREEN BEANS AND WALNUTS

*. . . and leeks, cucumber and carrots, with sesame oil adding a subtly delicious flavour. If you do not own a very large flameproof casserole, you may complete the cooking in a baking dish in the oven. Serve on brown rice for extra nourishment.*

45 ml (3 tbsp) sunflower oil
3-4 leeks, sliced
2-4 cloves garlic, crushed
200 g (7 oz) sliced green beans
3 sticks celery, sliced
sea salt and milled black pepper to taste
25 ml (5 tsp) sesame oil
45 ml (3 tbsp) sherry
1/2 cucumber, pared and julienned
florets from 1/2 cauliflower, coarse stems removed
4 young carrots, julienned
250 ml (8 fl oz) Marmite stock
25 ml (5 tsp) soy sauce
5 ml (1 tsp) ground ginger
20 ml (4 tsp) cornflour
125 g (4 oz) coarsely chopped walnuts
crumbled feta or grated Cheddar cheese for topping

Heat sunflower oil in large pan, add leeks, garlic, beans and celery and stir-fry for about 5 minutes. Remove to another pan or baking dish, season lightly and keep warm. Add sesame oil and sherry to pan, then add rest of vegetables. Lower heat and cook, half-covered, until tender-crisp, tossing occasionally. Mix all vegetables together in baking dish or saucepan.

Combine stock, soy sauce, ginger and cornflour. Stir into vegetables and add nuts. Cover and cook on medium heat, stirring occasionally and adding extra stock or water as necessary, until just done; or bake, covered, at 180°C (350°F, gas 4) for 20-30 minutes. Top each serving with chosen cheese.
*Serves 6.*

---

# BASIC VEGETABLE STIR-FRY SAUCE

*It is useful to have a basic sauce mixture to add flavour and succulence to a vegetable stir-fry. The following recipe may be used for 1 kg (2 1/4 lb) of mixed vegetables of choice. Once prepared (that is, washed, scrubbed or peeled, and sliced, chopped or julienned) they should be steamed or lightly poached until tender but still crisp; stir-frying is not necessary as oil is used in making the sauce.*

10 ml (2 tsp) dark sesame oil
15 ml (1 tbsp) sunflower oil
1-2 cloves garlic, crushed
1 bunch spring onions, chopped
1/2 knob root ginger, peeled and grated
375 ml (13 fl oz) vegetable stock or water
20 ml (4 tsp) cornflour
25 ml (5 tsp) sweet sherry
25 ml (5 tsp) soy sauce
1 kg (2 1/4 lb) vegetables of choice, steamed or poached

Heat both oils and sauté garlic, onions and ginger. Add stock or water. Slake cornflour with sherry and soy sauce, add to pan and stir until boiling and thickened. Pour into pan with the just-cooked and lightly seasoned vegetables and allow to boil up. Ladle over servings of brown rice and top with toasted, slivered almonds. Serve extra soy sauce separately, if desired.
*Serves 4.*

---

### GOMASIO
•

An Oriental seasoning salt: a marvellous condiment with the sesame seeds being rich in calcium, lecithin and unsaturated fats. It is best freshly made, but will keep for a few days stored in a sealed glass jar in the refrigerator.

**60 g (2 oz) husked sesame seeds**
**20 ml (4 tsp) sea salt**

Spread seeds in a non-stick frying pan and place on medium heat until golden brown. Shake pan occasionally and watch for burning. Remove, add salt, then pound, in batches, using a pestle and mortar. Do not pound to a pulp; the mixture should retain some texture.

# MUSHROOM AND SPROUT STIR-FRY

*This is a fine example of how to 'bake' a stir-fry.*

45 ml (3 tbsp) sunflower oil
plus a little extra
4 leeks, thinly sliced
1 small onion, chopped
2 sticks celery, sliced
2 medium carrots, julienned
2 cloves garlic, crushed
45 ml (3 tbsp) soy sauce
200 ml (7 fl oz) vegetable stock or water
20 ml (4 tsp) cornflour
a pinch of sugar
250 g (9 oz) mushrooms, wiped
and sliced
175 g (6 oz) shredded cabbage
1/2 cucumber, pared and cubed
60 g (2 oz) lentil sprouts
toasted almonds

In a large frying pan heat the oil and stir-fry leeks, onion, celery, carrots and garlic. After about 5 minutes on medium heat, transfer to a large, warmed dish and place in an oven preheated to 160°C (325°F, gas 3).

Mix the soy sauce, stock, cornflour and pinch of sugar. Put aside.

To pan add a dash more oil and mushrooms, cabbage and cucumber. Sauté until softened, stirring, then add lentil sprouts and soy sauce mixture. Cover and simmer for a few minutes, then mix into the other vegetables in the oven dish. Return to oven for about 10 minutes, then serve on rice and top with plenty of toasted almonds.
*Serves 4–6*

# QUICK-MIX STIR-FRY

*Although the bottom line in wholefood and vegetarian cookery always reads Fresh Ingredients, sometimes you don't have the time to prepare a mound of fresh vegetables. On these occasions, a packet of frozen vegetables is a boon. I have used several varieties with equal success; the stir-fry mixes are particularly good. Serve on a mixture of brown rice and lentils, cooked together for added convenience. For 200 g (7 oz) of each, you'll need just over 1 litre (1³/₄ pints) of salted water. Bring to the boil, then cover and simmer slowly until cooked and liquid is absorbed. Fork in a nut of butter and some chopped parsley. Top each serving generously with toasted almonds.*

30 ml (2 tbsp) each dark sesame and
sunflower oil
1 onion, chopped
2 leeks, sliced
2 cloves garlic, crushed
250 g (9 oz) brown mushrooms,
wiped and sliced
1 sprig rosemary needles, chopped
1 kg (2¹/₄ lb) frozen mixed vegetables
45 ml (3 tbsp) soy sauce
250 ml (8 fl oz) vegetable stock or water
45 ml (3 tbsp) sherry
25 ml (5 tsp) cornflour

Heat both oils in a large pan and sauté onion, leeks, garlic, mushrooms and rosemary. When softening, add the frozen vegetables and toss over medium heat until half-cooked. Mix together soy sauce, stock or water, sherry and cornflour. Add to pan, stir to mix, then cover and simmer for about 10 minutes until thickened and the vegetables are tender.
*Serves 6.*

# SPECIAL STIR-FRY

*I have called this a special stir-fry for two reasons: firstly, you use a frozen stir-fry mixture not ordinary frozen mixed vegetables (and this makes it especially convenient when time is short); secondly, it is one of the nicest ways in which to woo reluctant bean-eaters. Served on brown rice or pasta, it really is very good and extremely nutritious as well.*

25 ml (5 tsp) each sunflower and dark
sesame oil
500 g (18 oz) frozen stir-fry mixture
(preferably the one with mushrooms,
peas, leeks)
an extra 250 g (9 oz) brown mushrooms,
wiped and sliced
2 cloves garlic, crushed
1/2 fresh pineapple, sliced into rings
and diced
300 g (11 oz) cooked soya beans
500 ml (17 fl oz) vegetable stock or
Marmite stock
25 ml (5 tsp) sherry
30 ml (2 tbsp) cornflour
25 ml (5 tsp) soy sauce
10 ml (2 tsp) light brown sugar
5 ml (1 tsp) ground ginger
125 g (4 oz) lentil or mung bean sprouts
sea salt to taste
toasted, slivered almonds for garnish

Heat both oils in a large pan. Add frozen stir-fry mixture,* mushrooms and garlic and toss over medium heat until softening. Add pineapple and beans. Stir together stock, sherry, cornflour, soy sauce, sugar and ginger and add to pan. Bring to the boil, stirring, then cover and simmer over low heat for about 10 minutes — the mixture should be fairly thick, but juicy. Fork in sprouts, check seasoning (it will probably need a little salt) and serve, as suggested, with a sprinkling of almonds.
*Serves 6–8*

* If frozen mixture is icy and clumped together, place in a colander and hold under cold running water to separate. Pat dry and use immediately.

*Overleaf: Phyllo Parcels with Bean Sprouts, Feta and Almonds (p. 72) and Spinach Pancakes (p. 89).*

# MIDDLE EASTERN BUFFET

*Possibly the easiest and nicest way of feeding a crowd of vegetarians (or others with inquisitive palates) is to lay on a spread of salads, dips, pâtés and Pitta Bread (p. 93). The following recipes illustrate a few fine examples, to which you could add a hot dish, such as a Spinach and Feta Pie (p. 76) and a bowl of Tzatziki (p. 76). Although I have simplified the dips by using a processor, there is still a good deal of preparation involved in this type of meal as a wide variety of dishes is essential, but all the work can be done beforehand and the different colours and textures are a delight to the eye. Use your prettiest containers, the brightest of cloths, pots (rather than vases) of flowers and carafes of red wine.*

## HUMMUS

325 g (12 oz) cooked chickpeas
100 ml (7 tbsp) liquid from cooking
chickpeas or water
45 ml (3 tbsp) lemon juice
3 cloves garlic
45 ml (3 tbsp) tahini
45 ml (3 tbsp) olive oil
sea salt to taste
finely chopped parsley

Drain chickpeas, reserving 100 ml (7 tbsp) of cooking liquid. Using the grinding blade of a food processor, purée chickpeas, lemon juice, garlic, tahini and olive oil. With motor running, pour in reserved cooking liquid or water. The consistency should be that of thick mayonnaise. Add salt to taste, cover and chill. To serve, sprinkle with parsley and drizzle with a little olive oil.
*Makes about 300 g (11 oz).*

## TAHINI

· —

A rich and creamy paste (not unlike peanut butter) which is made from hulled, dried, roasted and ground sesame seeds, and is sold in cans or jars. Choose one made from pulped sesame seeds only, and which is free of preservatives and additives, and keep it refrigerated once opened. It really is worth experimenting with this delicious product, which is so popular in Middle Eastern cooking, but use it judiciously as it has a distinctive flavour. Try adding a little to sauces, mayonnaise or salad dressing.

Usually tahini separates and will be very thick at the bottom of the jar or can, so stir it very well, or spoon into a small bowl and whisk it until blended, then spoon out the required amount.

## BEAN AND SESAME PÂTÉ*

300 g (11 oz) cooked haricot beans,
well drained
45 ml (3 tbsp) tahini
20 ml (4 tsp) soy sauce
100 ml (7 tbsp) parsley sprigs
20 ml (4 tsp) lemon juice
6 slim spring onions, chopped
2 small cloves garlic
toasted sesame seeds for topping

Place all ingredients, except sesame seeds, in processor fitted with grinding blade. Process briefly. The mixture should not be absolutely smooth. Spoon into pottery container, cover and chill several hours, or overnight. Before serving, cover top generously with toasted sesame seeds.
*Makes about 500 g (18 oz).*

## BUTTER BEAN PÂTÉ WITH SHERRY*

20 ml (4 tsp) each dark sesame and
sunflower oil
2 cloves garlic
6-8 spring onions, chopped
2 × 400-g (14-oz) cans choice grade
butter beans, drained
20 ml (4 tsp) soy sauce
30 ml (2 tbsp) sweet sherry
30 g (1 oz) melted butter

Heat both oils in small pan and sauté garlic and onions. Tip into processor fitted with grinding blade. Add remaining ingredients except butter and process until smooth. Spoon into pottery container, prick holes all over with skewer, pour melted butter over and swirl in until thoroughly mixed. Cover and chill several hours or overnight.
*Makes about 500 g (18 oz).*

* These recipes can easily be halved.

## AUBERGINE AND RED PEPPER SALAD

*A version of the Yugoslavian ajivar, this is a simple salad using basic ingredients. If liked, 5 ml (1 tsp) dried oregano may be added when sautéeing the vegetables.*

800 g (1 lb 10 oz) aubergines
60 ml (4 tbsp) olive oil
2 red peppers, seeded and sliced into
thin strips
2 cloves garlic, crushed
2 leeks, thinly sliced
5 ml (1 tsp) sea salt and milled black
pepper to taste
20 ml (4 tsp) lemon juice
100 ml (7 tbsp) finely chopped parsley
natural yoghurt

Wash aubergines, remove bud ends, prick all over, place in baking dish and bake at 200°C (400°F, gas 6) until soft. When cool enough to handle, slice lengthways into four and ease out flesh. Discard skin, chop flesh into chunks, and place in salad bowl.

Heat oil and lightly sauté red peppers, garlic and leeks. Add to aubergines, plus any oil left in pan. Season mixture and add lemon juice and parsley. Use a fork to toss gently until combined, then cover and chill several hours. Before serving, drizzle yoghurt over the top.

## AUBERGINE SPREAD

575 g (1¼ lb) aubergines
5 ml (1 tsp) sea salt
4 spring onions, chopped
2 small cloves garlic
2.5 ml (½ tsp) each ground cumin
and coriander
25 ml (5 tsp) lemon juice
30 ml (2 tbsp) thick mayonnaise
a large pinch of sugar
2 hard-boiled eggs, chopped
finely chopped parsley or chives
for garnish

Wash aubergines, remove bud ends, prick all over, place in baking dish and bake at 200°C (400°F, gas 6) for 45-60 minutes until soft. When cool enough to handle, peel, cube and place in processor fitted with grinding blade. Add remaining ingredients, except eggs and garnish, and process until smooth. Spoon into a pottery bowl, fold in eggs, cover and chill several hours or overnight. Garnish with parsley or chives.
*Makes about 450 g (1 lb).*

## STUFFED VINE LEAVES

*Because the leaves are as fragile as phyllo pastry, I sometimes overlap two or three to hold the stuffing and seal any tears. The rice mixture will fill 20–25 parcels.*

200 g (7 oz) vine leaves in brine
25 ml (5 tsp) olive oil
1 small onion, chopped
200 g (7 oz) brown rice
75-100 ml (5-7 tbsp) sunflower seeds, preferably toasted
5 ml (1 tsp) dried dill
finely grated rind of half a lemon
60 ml (4 tbsp) currants (chopped, seedless raisins may be substituted)
2.5 ml (½ tsp) sea salt
750 ml (1¼ pints) vegetable stock or water
about 45 ml (3 tbsp) each sunflower and olive oil
25 ml (5 tsp) lemon juice

Drain and carefully separate vine leaves. Cut off any stems, place in a large bowl and cover with boiling water. Stand for 1 minute, then drain well.

Heat olive oil and sauté onion. Add rice and toss until coated with oil. Add sunflower seeds, dill, lemon rind, currants, salt and 500 ml (17 fl oz) of the stock or water. Stir with a fork to mix, then cover and cook on low heat for about 35 minutes until rice is almost done. Remove from stove and toss again, using a fork.

Lay leaves out flat and put about 30 ml (2 tbsp) rice mixture in the centre of each, using two or three leaves, as suggested. Flap over sides, then fold over into parcels. Place, seam side down, in baking dish to fit snugly, side by side.

Mix remaining stock, oil and lemon juice. Pour over parcels, cover securely, and bake at 160°C (325°F, gas 3) for 45 minutes or until plump and soft. Cool in liquid, then chill for several hours or overnight, but serve at room temperature.

## FELAFEL

*Traditionally, felafel are deep-fried in oil, but here they are simply baked.*

550 g (19 oz) cooked chickpeas, drained
2.5 ml (½ tsp) sea salt
45 ml (3 tbsp) finely chopped parsley
2 cloves garlic, crushed
5 ml (1 tsp) each ground cumin and coriander
25 ml (5 tsp) wholewheat flour
1 egg, beaten
oil for baking

Preheat oven to 180°C (350°F, gas 4). Grind chickpeas in food processor to a dry, mealy mixture. Put into bowl and add salt, parsley, garlic and spices. Sprinkle in flour and bind with egg, then roll into 15 small balls. Cover base of Swiss roll baking tin with a fairly generous layer of oil and heat in oven. Roll balls in hot oil, then bake for 20 minutes. Using a spatula, turn carefully. Raise heat to 220°C (425°F, gas 7) and bake for another 15 minutes or until crisp and brown. *Makes 15.*

## STUFFED GREEN PEPPERS

6 large green peppers
75 ml (5 tbsp) olive oil
1 onion, finely chopped
100 g (3½ oz) quick-cooking, long-grain white rice
2 large tomatoes, skinned, chopped and seeded
45 ml (3 tbsp) chopped parsley
2.5 ml (½ tsp) sea salt and milled black pepper to taste
5 ml (1 tsp) each dried dill and mint
20 ml (4 tsp) lemon juice

Cut a slice from stem end of peppers and reserve. Remove cores and seeds and rinse shells. Heat 30 ml (2 tbsp) of oil, add onion and fry lightly, then add rice, tomatoes, parsley, seasoning and herbs. Mix well, then cover and simmer very gently for 15 minutes. Spoon mixture loosely into peppers, about three-quarters full, and arrange upright in small pan with lid. Mix 250 ml (8 fl oz) hot water with remaining oil and lemon juice, pour over and around peppers, reposition tops, then cover pan and simmer slowly for about 45 minutes or until soft. If necessary, add a little water. When cooked, cool in pan, spooning juices over until cold. Chill well before serving.

## BABA GHANOUJ

*This is my version of this ethnic speciality. In the Middle East, it is usually served in one big bowl and diners scoop out servings with chunks of Pitta Bread (p. 93). The aubergines are sometimes charred, rather than baked, but personally I find the smoky flavour unpalatable.*

800 g (1 lb 10 oz) aubergines
5 ml (1 tsp) sea salt and milled black pepper to taste
2 cloves garlic
45 ml (3 tbsp) lemon juice
45 ml (3 tbsp) tahini
20 ml (4 tsp) olive oil
2.5 ml (½ tsp) each ground cumin and paprika
finely chopped parsley or chives or toasted sesame seeds for garnish

Wash aubergines, remove bud ends, prick well, place in baking dish and bake at 200°C (400°F, gas 6) for 45-60 minutes until soft. When cool enough to handle, peel and chop. Place pulp in processor fitted with grinding blade. Add remaining ingredients, except oil, spices and garnish, and process until smooth. Spoon into pottery bowl. Mix oil and spices, pour over top of mixture and using a skewer, swirl in until thoroughly combined. Cover and chill for several hours, or overnight. Garnish with parsley, chives or sesame seeds.
*Makes about 600 g (21 oz).*

## HARICOT BEAN SALAD (2)

*Simple bean salads (and stuffed peppers) are popular dishes in Greece and Turkey.*

600 g (21 oz) cooked haricot beans, well drained
45 ml (3 tbsp) lemon juice
100 ml (3½ fl oz) olive oil
2.5 ml (½ tsp) sea salt and milled black pepper to taste
5 ml (1 tsp) dried oregano
100 ml (7 tbsp) finely chopped parsley
2 tomatoes, diced
12 black olives, sliced
8 spring onions, chopped
feta cheese, rinsed and crumbled
3-4 hard-boiled eggs, sliced

Toss all ingredients, except cheese and eggs, until thoroughly mixed. Cover and chill several hours, or overnight. Before serving, top generously with feta cheese and garnish with hard-boiled eggs.

## STUFFED AUBERGINES

2 medium aubergines
1 large tomato, skinned and chopped
½ small onion, finely chopped
75 ml (5 tbsp) wholewheat breadcrumbs
25 ml (5 tsp) garlic blender mayonnaise
a little sea salt and milled black pepper to taste
2.5 ml (½ tsp) dried basil
a pinch of sugar
rinsed, crumbled feta cheese
25 ml (5 tsp) olive oil
black olives for garnish

Boil the aubergines in unsalted water for 8-10 minutes or until just softened. Cut in half and remove most of flesh, leaving the shells intact. Chop the pulp coarsely, and add the tomato, onion, breadcrumbs, mayonnaise, seasoning, basil and sugar. Fill shells and sprinkle with feta. Drizzle oil over the aubergines and bake, uncovered, at 160°C (325°F, gas 3) for 45 minutes. Leave to cool. The liquid will slowly be absorbed. Serve at room temperature garnished with olives.

*Aubergine and Red Pepper Salad (p. 84), Stuffed Aubergines (above), Baba Ghanouj (p. 85), Stuffed Green Peppers (p. 85), Felafel (p. 85), Hummus (p. 84), Stuffed Vine Leaves (p. 85), and Pitta Bread (p. 93).*

# GREEK GREEN BEAN AND AUBERGINE CASSEROLE

*An aromatic vegetable stew with a Plaka-type flavour and wonderful visual appeal. Serve on pasta, with Pitta Bread (p. 93) and a green salad, tossed with olive oil dressing and a few black olives.*

25 ml (5 tsp) each sunflower
and olive oil
1 large onion, chopped
1 green pepper, seeded and diced
3-4 cloves garlic, crushed
300 g (11 oz) aubergines, cubed
and dégorged
400 g (14 oz) young green beans,
trimmed and sliced
400 g (14 oz) fresh, juicy tomatoes,
skinned and chopped
2.5 ml (½ tsp) each dried oregano
and basil
1.25 ml (¼ tsp) dried thyme
2 bay leaves
100 ml (7 tbsp) chopped parsley
sea salt and milled black pepper to taste
5 ml (1 tsp) brown sugar
45 ml (3 tbsp) white wine
250 g (9 oz) feta cheese, rinsed and diced
for topping
toasted sesame seeds for topping

Heat oils in a large saucepan and lightly fry onion, green pepper and garlic. Add aubergines and beans, and sweat on low heat for a few minutes, tossing until vegetables are glistening. Add tomatoes, herbs, seasoning, sugar, 125 ml (4 fl oz) water and wine. Bring to the boil, then reduce heat, cover and cook slowly, stirring the mixture occasionally, until the vegetables are tender. Remove the bay leaves and, if necessary, bind the sauce with beurre manié (p. 53). Sprinkle with feta, top with sesame seeds, cover and heat through for 5 minutes; or spoon into a serving dish, add topping, and heat through in an oven.
*Serves 4.*

---

### SOURED CREAM
— • —

Unopened cartons should be stored upside down in the refrigerator. Once opened, spoon what hasn't been used into a glass jar with a lid, and keep refrigerated. Fresh cream and Bulgarian yoghurt are also best stored in glass jars when opened.

---

# STUFFED CHEESY AUBERGINES

*I hope, with this absolutely super recipe, to inspire restaurateurs to feature this dish on their menus. Although it is not difficult to prepare, the average cook, unused to exploring vegetarian meals, just might pass it over as being too fiddly, whereas diners, in search of an alternative to meat and fish, will surely love it: halved aubergines, stuffed with a mixture of vegetables, spiked with mustard, enriched with cream and blanketed with melting cheese, with chickpeas or beans tucked inside for a nutritional boost.*

2 aubergines, weighing
300 g (11 oz) each
45 ml (3 tbsp) olive oil
25 ml (5 tsp) sunflower oil
1 small onion, finely chopped
1-2 cloves garlic, finely chopped
2.5 ml (½ tsp) mixed dried herbs
250 g (9 oz) baby marrows, pared, sliced
thinly lengthways and diced
45 ml (3 tbsp) soured cream
175 g (6 oz) cooked chickpeas or soya or
haricot beans or a mixture of chickpeas
and beans (depending on what
you have on hand)
5 ml (1 tsp) prepared mustard
2.5 ml (½ tsp) sea salt
plenty of sliced Mozzarella or
low-fat cheese

Wash aubergines, remove bud ends and slice in half lengthways. Score the flesh lightly in a diamond pattern, sprinkle with some sea salt and stand for 30 minutes. Rinse off the salt and pat the aubergines dry.

Heat olive oil and 25 ml (5 tsp) water in a large frying pan with a lid. Add aubergines, cut side down, and cook gently, covered, until just tender but not wrinkled or collapsed — for about 25 minutes. A dash of extra water may be necessary if moisture evaporates too quickly. Place shells in baking dish to fit fairly closely, and when cool enough to handle, scoop out most of the pulp with a grapefruit spoon or knife, leaving a firm shell. Reserve the pulp.

Heat the sunflower oil in the same pan, add onion, garlic, herbs and marrows, then cover and cook gently until soft. Add cream, chickpeas/beans, mustard, salt and reserved aubergine pulp. Mix well and then spoon into aubergine shells, mounding high. Top each 'mountain' with plenty of cheese, then bake at 180°C (350°F, gas 4) for 30 minutes.
*Serves 4.*

---

# GREEK VEGETABLE CASSEROLE WITH BEANS AND FETA

*Serve this delicious medley of Mediterranean-type vegetables on brown rice with a lettuce and avocado salad tossed in garlicky French dressing.*

25 ml (5 tsp) each sunflower
and olive oil
1 large onion, chopped
2 leeks, sliced
1 green pepper, seeded and diced
2 cloves garlic, crushed
1 aubergine, weighing 250 g (9 oz),
cubed and dégorged
6 baby marrows, total weight 250 g
(9 oz), pared and sliced
4 large, juicy tomatoes, skinned
and chopped
450 g (1 lb) cooked soya or haricot beans
5 ml (1 tsp) sea salt and milled black
pepper to taste
5 ml (1 tsp) each dried oregano and basil
5 ml (1 tsp) sugar
250 ml (8 fl oz) vegetable stock or 5 ml
(1 tsp) Marmite in 250 ml (8 fl oz) water
black olives, sliced
200-250 g (7-9 oz) feta cheese, rinsed
and coarsely crumbled

Heat oils in a large pan and sauté onion, leeks, green pepper and garlic. When softened, add aubergine, marrows and tomatoes. Cover and sweat for 5 minutes over low heat. Add drained beans, seasoning, herbs, sugar and stock. Stir to mix, then turn into large baking dish. Bake, covered, at 150°C (300°F, gas 2) for 1¼ hours, stirring once or twice and adding more liquid if needed.

Before serving, add olives and sprinkle with feta. Return to oven to heat through.
*Serves 4–6.*

---

### AUBERGINES
— • —

It is much better to buy several small aubergines, which, if fresh and young enough, don't need dégorging. This is a process by means of which the bitter juices are extracted. Wash aubergines, slice or cube them, place in colander, salt quite heavily, and put weight on top. Leave for 30-45 minutes, then rinse and dry. Drying is important, to avoid adding excess liquid to the dish. Use either a salad spinner or kitchen paper towels.

# SPINACH PANCAKES

*Also called Crêpes Florentine, this dish takes a while to assemble, but can be prepared in advance and baked when required. The pancake batter (which makes lacy, light crêpes) and the cheese sauce are both made in a blender, which cuts down on preparation time.*

### CRÊPES
125 g (4 oz) white or sifted brown flour
1.25 ml (¼ tsp) sea salt
1 egg plus 1 yolk
250 ml (8 fl oz) milk
125 ml (4 fl oz) water
25 ml (5 tsp) sunflower oil

### FILLING
500 g (18 oz) frozen spinach, thawed
1.25 ml (¼ tsp) sea salt
1.25 ml (¼ tsp) freshly grated nutmeg

### SAUCE
600 ml (1 pint) milk
45 ml (3 tbsp) white or 60 ml (4 tbsp) brown flour
125 g (4 oz) Gruyère cheese, grated
2.5 ml (½ tsp) each dry mustard and sea salt
45 g (1½ oz) soft butter

grated Parmesan (or Cheddar or Gruyère) cheese and paprika

Put all the ingredients for the crêpes into blender, blend well and leave to stand for at least 30 minutes. The consistency should be creamy and medium-thick, and the batter will make 10 crêpes, 18-20 cm (7-8 in) in diameter. Stack, after cooking, interleaved with sheets of greaseproof paper.

For the filling, cook spinach, drain very well in colander, and press out all moisture. Season with salt and nutmeg.

For sauce, put 500 ml (17 fl oz) of the milk, the chosen flour, Gruyère cheese, mustard, salt and butter into blender, blend well and then pour into saucepan and cook over low heat, stirring, until thick and cheese has melted. Stir 125 ml (4 fl oz) of the sauce into the spinach purée and mix well. Fill each crêpe with a large spoonful of the purée and roll into cigar shapes. Place close together in a shallow, buttered baking dish.

Thin the remaining cheese sauce with the remaining milk and pour over crêpes. Sprinkle generously with Parmesan cheese (or Cheddar or Gruyère if preferred) and dust with paprika. Bake at 180°C (350°F, gas 4) for 30 minutes.
*Serves 10 as a starter or 5 as a main course.*

# CRÊPES RATATOUILLE

*In this dish, pancakes are wrapped round a savoury vegetable filling, covered with a white sauce, sprinkled with a topping of cheese, and then baked. This dish can be assembled successfully in advance.*

### BLENDER CRÊPES
125 g (4 oz) white or sifted brown flour
1.25 ml (¼ tsp) sea salt
1 egg
250 ml (8 fl oz) milk
125 ml (4 fl oz) water
25 ml (5 tsp) sunflower oil
2.5 ml (½ tsp) dried oregano (optional)

### FILLING
15 ml (1 tbsp) each sunflower and olive oil
1 medium aubergine, cubed
1 green pepper, seeded and diced
1 onion, chopped
200 g (7 oz) small baby marrows, scrubbed and sliced
sea salt and milled black pepper to taste
2 large tomatoes, skinned and chopped
2 cloves garlic, crushed
5 ml (1 tsp) dried basil
5 ml (1 tsp) sugar

### SAUCE
a knob of butter
25 ml (5 tsp) sunflower oil
45 ml (3 tbsp) white flour or 60 ml (4 tbsp) brown flour
500 ml (17 fl oz) milk
sea salt and black pepper to taste
5 ml (1 tsp) prepared mustard

### TOPPING
grated Cheddar or Gruyère cheese
25 ml (5 tsp) grated Parmesan

Put all ingredients for crêpes into a blender and blend well, stopping to scrape down sides once or twice. Stand for 1 hour, blend again, then make thin crêpes in an 18-cm (7-in) frying pan. As they are done, stack on large plate with a circle of greaseproof paper between the crêpes.

For the filling, put oils, aubergine, green pepper, onion, baby marrows and seasoning into a large saucepan. Cover and stew slowly, stirring occasionally, for about 35 minutes or until soft. Add tomatoes, garlic, basil and sugar. Half-cover saucepan and cook until tomatoes are pulpy. If necessary, remove lid and boil rapidly to reduce excess liquid. Cool, then divide between crêpes, roll into cigar shapes and place side by side in buttered baking dish. The filling is enough for 8-10 crêpes.

Make white sauce by melting butter with oil, stirring in flour, then adding milk slowly, stirring constantly. When thick, add seasonings and pour over crêpes. Sprinkle generously with Cheddar, top with Parmesan and heat through at 160°C (325°F, gas 3) for about 40 minutes.
*Serve 1–2 crêpes per person.*

# BREADS & ROLLS

## WHOLEWHEAT BUTTERMILK BREAD

*A reliable version of this favourite loaf. The quantity of bicarbonate of soda used is small, but it is enough for the batter to rise without imparting the sometimes overt bicarb flavour.*

500 g (18 oz) wholewheat flour
5 ml (1 tsp) sea salt
5 ml (1 tsp) bicarbonate of soda
15 ml (1 tbsp) sunflower oil
15 ml (1 tbsp) honey or molasses or brown sugar
75 g (2½ oz) seedless raisins (optional)
500 ml (17 fl oz) buttermilk or natural drinking yoghurt
sesame seeds for topping

Mix flour and salt. Sift in the bicarbonate of soda (this is important). Add oil, honey and raisins, if using. Stir to mix and then pour in buttermilk or yoghurt. Stir, using a wooden spoon, until ingredients are thoroughly combined — the batter will be soft and sticky. Turn into an oiled 20 × 13 × 7.5-cm (8 × 5 × 3-in) loaf tin, sprinkle with sesame seeds and make a slight depression down the centre of the loaf.

Bake on 180°C (350°F, gas 4) for 1 hour. Stand for 5 minutes, then turn out and return to oven for 5 minutes to crisp the sides. Cool on a wire rack.
*Makes 1 loaf.*

### VARIATION

*Replace 150 g (5 oz) of the wholewheat flour with muesli. Avoid using muesli containing sunflower seeds as these will turn green in this bread.*

*Wholewheat Soda Bread with Rosemary (p. 94).*

# INSTANT WHOLEWHEAT BATTER BREAD

*This is the perfect bread for reluctant bakers — no kneading required.*

**375 g (13 oz) wholewheat flour**
**125 g (4 oz) white bread flour**
**100 ml (7 tbsp) crushed wheat**
**7.5 ml (1½ tsp) instant dry yeast**
**5 ml (1 tsp) sea salt**
**100 ml (7 tbsp) sunflower seeds**
**25 ml (5 tsp) sunflower oil**
**25 ml (5 tsp) honey**
**about 450 ml (¾ pint) warm water**
**extra sunflower seeds for topping**

Mix flours, crushed wheat, yeast, salt and sunflower seeds. Mix in oil and honey. Add 300 ml (½ pint) of the water, then stir in just enough of remaining water to make a soft, sticky dough. Mix well, then turn into an oiled 23 × 13 × 7.5-cm (9 × 5 × 3-in) loaf tin, sprinkle with sunflower seeds, pressing in lightly, and leave to rise in a warm place until 1-2 cm (½-¾ in) over top of tin. Cover, if liked, with a large plastic bag, allowing it to balloon over the top so that it does not stick to the rising dough.

Remove bag and bake on middle shelf of oven at 200°C (400°F, gas 6) for 30 minutes and then at 180°C (350°F, gas 4) for 20-30 minutes. Turn out on to a wire rack to cool. *Makes 1 medium loaf.*

# ENRICHED BATTER BREAD

*A delicious loaf, packed with healthy ingredients. It rises well, has an even, flat top and slices neatly.*

**25 ml (5 tsp) honey**
**475 ml (16 fl oz) warm water**
**10 ml (2 tsp) dried yeast**
**375 g (13 oz) wholewheat flour**
**60 g (2 oz) crushed wheat**
**75 ml (5 tbsp) soya flour**
**75 ml (5 tbsp) fat-free milk powder**
**100 ml (7 tbsp) wheatgerm**
**125 g (4 oz) brown bread flour**
**7.5 ml (1½ tsp) sea salt**
**25 ml (5 tsp) sunflower oil**
**sunflower seeds for topping**

Dissolve the honey in 125 ml (4 fl oz) of the warm water. Sprinkle in the yeast, cover and then leave to froth.

Mix the remaining ingredients (except the sunflower seeds). Give the frothy yeast a quick stir, and then pour it into a well in centre of dry ingredients. Mix, using a wooden spoon, and gradually add the remaining water, or just enough to make a thick, sticky batter.

Turn the batter into an oiled loaf tin measuring 23 × 13 × 7.5 cm (9 × 5 × 3 in), which should be nearly two-thirds full. Sprinkle the top thickly with sunflower seeds, pressing them in lightly. Leave to rise in a warm place for 45-60 minutes.

Bake at 200°C (400°F, gas 6) for 15 minutes, then at 180°C (350°F, gas 4) for 45-60 minutes. Stand a few minutes, run a knife round the edges and turn out on to a wire rack to cool.
*Makes 1 loaf.*

# NUTTY BROWN BLOOMER LOAF

*A beautiful bread, incorporating two flours, wheatgerm and sunflower seeds, and as professional-looking as anything you can buy. It requires only one rising, which is quite lengthy due to the unrefined ingredients, but it is nevertheless easy to make and is tops on the taste test.*

**375 g (13 oz) wholewheat flour**
**10 ml (2 tsp) sea salt**
**15 ml (1 tbsp) instant dry yeast**
**350 ml (11 fl oz) warm water**
**25 ml (5 tsp) honey**
**25 ml (5 tsp) sunflower oil**
**225 g (8 oz) white bread flour**
**60 g (2 oz) wheatgerm**
**60 g (2 oz) sunflower seeds**
**milk for brushing dough**
**melted butter for brushing top of bread**

In a large mixing bowl combine 175 g (6 oz) of the wholewheat flour, the sea salt and the yeast. Mix together the water, honey and oil. Stir into the flour mixture and mix to a sloppy dough. Cover and leave to rest for 10 minutes. Add the remaining wholewheat flour, the white flour, wheatgerm and sunflower seeds. Mix with a wooden spoon and then with your hands to form a dough, adding up to 75 ml (2½ fl oz) warm water if necessary. Knead in the bowl for 8-10 minutes — this is a firm dough which requires some hard kneading. When the mixture forms a smooth ball and leaves the sides of the bowl clean, shape the dough into a 25 × 13-cm (10 × 5-in) bloomer (or slab) with blunt ends.

Place on an oiled baking tray and tuck two cloths tightly on either side so that the dough rises upward rather than sideways. Make six deep diagonal slashes across the top, then leave to rise for about 1 hour or until doubled. Brush with milk.

Bake the bread at 200°C (400°F, gas 6) for 30 minutes. Cool on a wire rack, then brush the top with melted butter for a shiny finish.
*Makes 1 loaf.*

# HERBY OAT BATTER BREAD

*No kneading required for this wholesome, crunchy loaf perfumed with fresh rosemary.*

about 375 ml (13 fl oz) warm water
5 ml (1 tsp) sugar
10 ml (2 tsp) dried yeast
200 g (7 oz) wholewheat flour
100 g (3½ oz) white bread flour
90 g (3 oz) crushed wheat
90 g (3 oz) rolled oats
5 ml (1 tsp) sea salt
3-4 cloves garlic, crushed
25 ml (5 tsp) finely chopped fresh
rosemary needles
25 ml (5 tsp) sunflower oil
25 ml (5 tsp) honey

Pour 250 ml (8 fl oz) of the water into a jug. Stir in sugar, sprinkle in yeast, then cover and stand until frothy — for about 15 minutes. Mix flours, crushed wheat, oats, salt, garlic and rosemary. Stir oil and honey into yeast mixture, then add to flour mixture. Mix, and then slowly stir in remaining water or enough to make a sloppy dough. When well combined, turn into an oiled 20 × 10 × 6-cm (8 × 4 × 2½-in) loaf tin. Smooth the top, then leave to rise in a warm place until 1 cm (½ in) over the top of the tin — for about 45 minutes.

Bake at 200°C (400°F, gas 6) for 30 minutes, then at 180°C (350°F, gas 4) for 20-25 minutes. Stand for 1 minute, run a knife round the edges and turn out on to a wire rack to cool. Brush top with melted butter.
*Makes 1 loaf.*

# FOUR-SEED BATTER BREAD

*A nutritious, crunchy, flat-topped loaf, excellent for sandwiches as it slices so well.*

25 ml (5 tsp) honey
550 ml (18 fl oz) warm water
15 ml (1 tbsp) dried yeast
500 g (18 oz) wholewheat flour
125 g (4 oz) white bread flour
45 ml (3 tbsp) each sesame seeds
and linseeds
45 g (1½ oz) sunflower seeds
5 ml (1 tsp) sea salt
poppy seeds for topping

Mix honey into 250 ml (8 fl oz) of the warm water and stir to dissolve. Sprinkle in the yeast, cover and leave to froth. Mix flours, sesame seeds, linseeds, sunflower seeds and salt. Stir the risen yeast, pour it into a well in the centre of the flour mixture, stir, then slowly add the remaining water, or just enough to make a sticky but quite stiff dough. Pat firmly into an oiled 23 × 13 × 7.5-cm (9 × 5 × 3-in) loaf tin, sprinkle the top with poppy seeds, and leave the dough to rise in a warm place for 1 hour or until it is just over the top of the tin.

Bake at 200°C (400°F, gas 6) for 30 minutes, and then at 180°C (350°F, gas 4) for 20-30 minutes. Run a knife round the sides and leave the bread in the tin for 1 minute before turning out on to a wire rack to cool.
*Makes 1 loaf.*

# MUFFIN TIN WHOLEWHEAT ROLLS

*A basic wholewheat batter is used for these quickly-made muffin-shaped 'rolls'.*

500-550 ml (17-18 fl oz) warm water
a pinch of sugar
10 ml (2 tsp) dried yeast
375 g (13 oz) wholewheat flour
125 g (4 oz) white bread flour
90-175 g (3-6 oz) seedless raisins
(optional)
100 ml (7 tbsp) rolled oats
5 ml (1 tsp) sea salt
25 ml (5 tsp) sunflower oil
25 ml (5 tsp) honey or half honey,
half molasses
60 g (2 oz) sunflower seeds
extra sunflower seeds or crushed wheat
for topping

Mix 250 ml (8 fl oz) of the water with a pinch of sugar. Sprinkle in yeast, cover and leave to froth. Mix remaining ingredients, except sunflower seeds and crushed wheat for topping, in a large bowl. Stir frothy yeast and pour into well in centre of dry ingredients. Mix, and then slowly stir in remaining warm water or just enough to make a thick, moist dough. Spoon into large, oiled muffin tins — they should be just over halfway filled with batter. Top with extra sunflower seeds or crushed wheat pressed in lightly. Leave to rise in a warm place until batter rises (will be slightly humped) to just over the tops of the tins — for 50-60 minutes.

Bake at 200°C (400°F, gas 6) for about 25 minutes, until browned and firm. Stand for a few minutes and then run a knife round the edges to loosen. Cool on a wire rack, and eat freshly baked.
*Makes 14–16 large rolls.*

# PITTA BREAD

*Much experimenting has resulted in what are, to my mind, quite the best of home-made pittas. Fun to make, the shaping is quite different from that of ordinary bread rolls. They rise in the oven like fat little cushions and form perfect pockets for stuffing. A high baking temperature is important and to ensure the formation of pockets, the dough should not be creased when rolling or pinched when turned over just prior to baking.*

10 ml (2 tsp) sugar
300 ml (½ pint) warm water
10 ml (2 tsp) dried yeast
500 g (18 oz) plain flour
5 ml (1 tsp) sea salt
30 ml (2 tbsp) sunflower oil

Stir sugar into water. Sprinkle in yeast, cover and leave to froth.

Sift the flour and salt into a large bowl. Add the oil. Stir the bubbly yeast and pour it into a well in centre of the dry ingredients. Combine, using a wooden spoon, and then mix to a dough with your hands, adding about 45 ml (3 tbsp) extra water, or enough to make a kneadable dough. Turn the dough on to lightly floured board and knead well for 10 minutes until the mixture forms a pliable ball. Return to bowl, brush the top of the dough with oil, cover the bowl with a kitchen towel and leave the dough to rise for about 1 hour or until doubled.

Punch down the dough and pinch off ten equal pieces. Roll them into balls between the palms of your hands, rest for 5 minutes and then, using a rolling pin, roll the dough into thin ovals. Place the ovals on ungreased baking trays dusted with cake flour. Leave to prove, uncovered, for about 30 minutes until they are puffy and doubled in thickness. Turn over carefully and sift a little flour over them.

Bake, a tray at a time, just above the centre of the oven at 240°C (475°F, gas 9) for 7 minutes. Remove from oven and wrap in a cloth to soften. Slice off the tops and press the sides gently to open out pockets.
*Makes 10.*

### WHOLEWHEAT PITTA BREAD

*Use 250 g (9 oz) white bread flour and 250 g (9 oz) wholewheat flour. Sift the white flour with 5 ml (1 tsp) salt, add the wholewheat flour, then proceed as for white pittas. A little extra water may be necessary, but the rising and proving times are about the same.*

If you process butter and oil, you get a creamy mixture which spreads like margarine, but retains the natural flavour and goodness of butter. The addition of sunflower oil makes healthy good sense as it contains a high proportion of unsaturated fatty acids. Make a big batch, keep some on hand in the refrigerator, and freeze the rest.

**500 g (18 oz) soft, unsalted butter, diced**
**5 ml (1 tsp) sea salt**
**200-250 ml (7-8 fl oz) sunflower oil**

Place butter and salt in processor fitted with the grinding blade, and process to a soft paste. Slowly dribble in the oil, keeping the motor running. If necessary, stop and run a spatula round the sides, then continue blending until well mixed. The mixture will be sloppy. Turn into fridge containers. Keep chilled.

For Herby Mock Butter, follow the above recipe, but add the following to the butter and salt:

**a few tufts of parsley**
**16 large, fresh basil leaves**
**4 sprigs each oregano and marjoram, leaves only**
**2 cloves garlic**
**4 sage leaves**

Process the herbs and garlic to chop, with the butter and salt, before adding the oil.

## WHOLEWHEAT HONEY BREAD

*A lovely, malt-coloured health loaf using instant yeast. Apart from simplifying mixing, instant yeast also cuts down on rising time.*

15 ml (1 tbsp) instant dry yeast
100 ml (7 tbsp) wheatgerm
500 g (18 oz) wholewheat flour
90 g (3 oz) seedless raisins
5 ml (1 tsp) sea salt
100 ml (7 tbsp) sunflower seeds
about 500 ml (17 fl oz) warm water
45 ml (3 tbsp) honey
15 ml (1 tbsp) sunflower oil

Mix yeast, wheatgerm, flour, raisins, salt and sunflower seeds in a large mixing bowl. Whisk 250 ml (8 fl oz) of water with honey and oil. Pour into dry ingredients and mix, then add remaining water, or enough to make a batter with consistency of a fruit cake. Turn into an oiled 23 × 13 × 7.5-cm (9 × 5 × 3-in) loaf tin. Leave in a warm place until batter rises to just over top of tin — for about 30 minutes. Bake at 200°C (400°F, gas 6) for 30 minutes, then at 180°C (350°F, gas 4) for 20 minutes. Turn out on to a wire rack to cool.
*Makes 1 large loaf.*

## WHOLEWHEAT SODA BREAD WITH ROSEMARY

*Soda bread is a traditional Scottish bread served on Burns Night with Finnan Haddie Soup and Haggis. Flavoured with fresh rosemary, this version makes a lovely, perfumed bread. Serve freshly baked, broken into quarters, with butter.*

250 g (9 oz) plain flour
5 ml (1 tsp) each sea salt, bicarbonate of soda and sugar
250 g (9 oz) wholewheat flour
15 ml (1 tbsp) finely chopped fresh rosemary needles
30 g (1 oz) butter
about 400 ml (14 fl oz) buttermilk
beaten egg or milk for topping

Sift flour, salt and bicarbonate of soda. Add sugar, flour and rosemary. Rub in butter. Add buttermilk and mix to a soft dough. Shape into two 15-cm (6-in) rounds and place on a floured baking tray. Using back of knife, score deeply into quarters. Brush tops with egg (or milk, but egg gives a better colour). Bake at 200°C (400°F, gas 6) for 30 minutes.
*Makes 2 loaves.*

## OAT, RYE AND CARAWAY BATTER BREAD

about 400 ml (14 fl oz) warm water
5 ml (1 tsp) sugar
10 ml (2 tsp) dried yeast
250 g (9 oz) wholewheat flour
150 g (5 oz) rye flour
90 g (3 oz) rolled oats
5 ml (1 tsp) sea salt
5 ml (1 tsp) caraway seeds
25 ml (5 tsp) sunflower oil
25 ml (5 tsp) honey

TOPPING
45 ml (3 tbsp) sunflower seeds
2.5 ml (½ tsp) caraway seeds

Pour 250 ml (8 fl oz) of the water into a jug. Stir in sugar, sprinkle in the yeast, then cover and stand until frothy — for about 15 minutes.

Mix flours, oats, salt and caraway seeds. Stir oil and honey into yeast mixture, then add to flour mixture. Mix, then slowly stir in remaining water, or enough to make a sloppy dough. When well combined, turn into oiled 20 × 10 × 6-cm (8 × 4 × 2½-in) loaf tin. Smooth top and sprinkle with topping. Leave to rise in warm place until 1 cm (½ in) over top of tin — for about 45 minutes.

Bake at 200°C (400°F, gas 6) for 30 minutes, then at 180°C (350°F, gas 4) for 20-25 minutes. Stand for a minute, run a knife round the edges and turn out on to a wire rack to cool.
*Makes 1 loaf.*

Sliced bread, baked with a topping of herb butter mixed with Parmesan cheese and sesame seeds, makes a delicious accompaniment to many Mediterranean-style dishes, and affords a welcome change from the usual garlic French loaf. Use a fat, crusty white loaf — definitely not ordinary white bread — and cut into 2-cm (¾-in) slices.

**250 g (9 oz) soft butter**
**3-4 cloves garlic, crushed**
**a few grinds of black pepper**
**45 ml (3 tbsp) grated Parmesan cheese**
**45 ml (3 tbsp) dehusked sesame seeds**
**5 ml (1 tsp) dried marjoram**
**oil for brushing pan**

Mash butter with rest of ingredients. Brush a large baking tray with oil, lay bread slices on it, spread with half butter mixture, then turn over and repeat. Bake at 160°C (325°F, gas 3) for 20 minutes, turn slices, and bake until golden brown. Alternatively, toast bread on one side, spread the other side generously with butter mixture, then grill until bubbling.) Serve hot.

*Pitta Bread (p. 93), Four-Seed Batter Bread (p. 93) and Muffin Tin Wholewheat Rolls (p. 93).*

# INDEX